FEEDBACK

A NEW FRAMEWORK FOR MACROECONOMIC POLICY

ADVANCED STUDIES IN THEORETICAL AND APPLIED ECONOMETRICS VOLUME 10

Books by David Andrew Kendrick

Programming Investment in the Process Industries

Notes and Problems in Microeconomic Theory (with Samuel Bowles and Peter Dixon)

The Planning of Industrial Programs (with Ardy Stoutjesdijk)

Stochastic Control for Economic Models

The Planning of Investment Programs in the Steel Industry (with Alexander Meeraus and Jaime Alatorre)

GAMS: An Introduction (with Alexander Meeraus)

A complete list of this series is on the final page.

FEEDBACK
A NEW FRAMEWORK FOR MACROECONOMIC POLICY

by

David A. Kendrick

1988 **KLUWER ACADEMIC PUBLISHERS**
a member of the KLUWER ACADEMIC PUBLISHERS GROUP
DORDRECHT / BOSTON / LANCASTER

Distributors

for the United States and Canada: Kluwer Academic Publishers, 101 Philip Drive, Norwell, MA 02061, USA
for the UK and Ireland: Kluwer Academic Publishers, MTP Press Limited, Falcon House, Queen Square, Lancaster LA1 1RN, UK
for all other countries: Kluwer Academic Publishers Group, Distribution Center, P.O. Box 322, 3300 AH Dordrecht, The Netherlands

Library of Congress Cataloging in Publication Data

Kendrick, David A.
Feedback : a new framework for macroeconomic policy / by David A. Kendrick..
p. cm. -- (Advanced studies in theoretical and applied econometrics ; v. 10)
Bibliography: p.
Includes index.

1. Macroeconomics--Econometric models. 2. Control theory.
I. Title. II. Series.
HB172.5.K45 1987
339.5--dc19 87-20990
CIP

ISBN -13:978-94-010-7733-0 e-ISBN:978-94-009-2746-9
DOI:10.1007/978-94-009-2746-9

Copyright

Preface

In the past fifteen years a new field of research has emerged in economics: the application of control theory methods to macroeconomics and to microeconomics. The papers and books which have resulted from this research are important to the development of theoretical and applied economics. However, they are inaccessible to many with interest in economics because of the technical nature of the discussion. This book attempts to make the macroeconomic portion of this literature more accessible by providing a discussion of the key issues using words and figures rather than mathematical symbols.

I would like to thank my mentors and colleagues in control theory and economics for their help over the years: Masanao Aoki, Michael Athans, Yaakov Bar-Shalom, Jeremy Bray, Arthur Bryson, Gregory Chow, Ray Fair, Laurie Henrikson, David Livesey, Raman Mehra, Alfred Norman, Robert Pindyck, Franklin Shupp, John Taylor, Lance Taylor, Peter Tinsley, Edison Tse, and Stephen Turnovsky.

In addition, I appreciate the help of Nancy McMeans

Richey who provided comments and suggestions on two drafts of this book. I would also like to thank the University Research Institute of the University of Texas at Austin for support during a sabbatical leave when much of this manuscript was written. Finally, I would like to thank the following individuals who read all or part of an earlier version of the manuscript and provided comments on it: Bob Andrews, Michael Athans, William Bard, Yaakov Bar-Shalom, Jeremy Bray, Gregory Chow, Jae-Ho Chung, Paul Coomes, Roger Craine, Douglas Dacy, Mario DePillis, Greg DeCoster, Valerie Dunnam, Ray Fair, Andy Hughes Hallet, Charles Kindleberger, Robert Pindyck, Congressman Dan Rostenkowski, Walt Rostow, Berc Rustem, Franklin Shupp, Robert Solow, Lester Thurow, Peter Tinsley, James Tobin, Edison Tse, Jon Wainwright, and Piyu Yue.

Contents

1
Introduction

A lunar lander approaches the moon and settles gently onto that dusty surface. A giant commercial aircraft crossing the Atlantic in a storm is blown off course and is smoothly brought back by the plane's automatic pilot. The temperature in a Chicago town house drops on a cold winter night but is quickly and quietly restored as the furnace clicks on. All of these are examples of feedback control systems. The radar on the lunar lander feeds back the distance to the moon's surface and the blast of the rockets is adjusted. The navigational equipment feeds back latitude and longitude to the automatic pilot on the plane and the course is corrected. The thermostat records a drop in temperature and the furnace is turned on.

Each of these familiar objects — a lunar lander, a plane, a furnace — is a dynamic system, a system that is designed to reach a target or to follow a desired path through space or time. So too is the economy a dynamic system. It is a dynamic system with targets and desired paths — low unemployment and inflation and a small government deficit. It is a dynamic system with lags — tax cuts proposed today require many months to be approved and put into effect. It is a dynamic system beset with uncertainty from oil shocks and droughts.

These characteristics of the economy — goals, dynamics, uncertainty — make it a dynamic system that can be analyzed with the same mathematical and computational tools used for lunar landers, airplanes, and thermostats. Such is the subject of this book — a study of the application of feedback control methods to macroeconomic policy determination.

Feedback is a familiar idea in economics. It is as familiar as unemployment compensation. As is illustrated in Figure 1.1, when unemployment rises unemployment compensation rises, and this provides an increase in income, which then mitigates the unemployment.

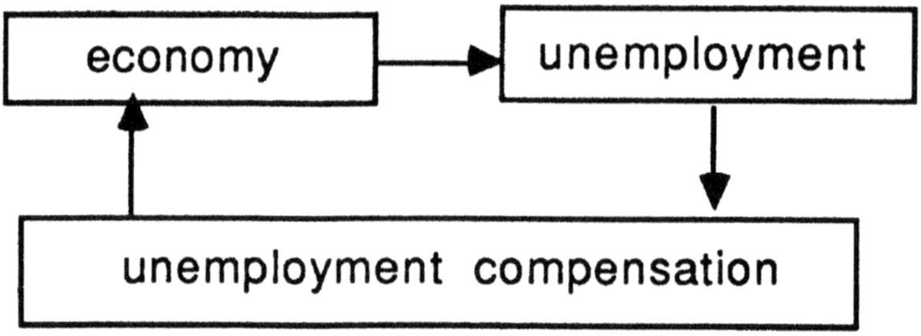

Figure 1.1. Feedback through unemployment compensation

Therefore an increase in unemployment sets in motion feedback that works through the unemployment system to decrease unemployment and stabilize the economy.

So feedback is a familiar idea, but the framework of feedback control systems developed in engineering is not yet widely known in economics. Like the characteristics of the economy mentioned above, the feedback framework consists of

- goals
- dynamics
- uncertainty.

The goals are low unemployment, low inflation, a balanced budget, high growth rates, an equitable income distribution, and balanced exports and imports. These goals of the policymakers become desired paths for the economy in a dynamic setting. For example, if unemployment is high at the beginning of an administration, the desired path may be a gradual decrease in the unemployment rate over time. Similarly a desired path for the deficit may be a high deficit at the beginning of a new administration and a lower deficit as the next election approaches.

The dynamics are of two types — decision lags and effect lags. Decision lags are the time between an adverse change in the economy and a decision to do something about it. For example, decision lags extend (1) from the time unemployment rises until the President proposes and Congress passes a tax cut or an expenditure increase or (2) from the time unemployment rises until the Federal Reserve Board increases the money supply in order to drive down interest rates.

Effect lags cover the period between the time a government action is taken and the economy responds. For example, effect lags extend from the time taxes are decreased until consumers begin to spend the additional disposable income, employers hire more workers, and the unemployment rate drops.

Uncertainty comes in many forms but three types will be singled out for special treatment in the feedback framework. These kinds of uncertainty are

- shocks
- behavior
- measurement.

Shocks are unexpected events like oil price increases or crop failures. Behavioral uncertainty is the uncertain response of agents in the economy to changes in policy; for example, the response of consumers to a tax increase or the response of entrepreneurs to a decrease in the investment tax credit. Measurement uncertainty is used to indicate that our knowledge of the state of the economy is less than perfect. For example the national income accounts are revised as additional data is obtained and the measurement error is decreased.

If the elements of the feedback framework are used to determine policy then what is the form of the policies? The policies are feedback rules like, "the condition of the economy is fed back to determine economic policy."

For example, the unemployment rate is fed back to determine unemployment compensation

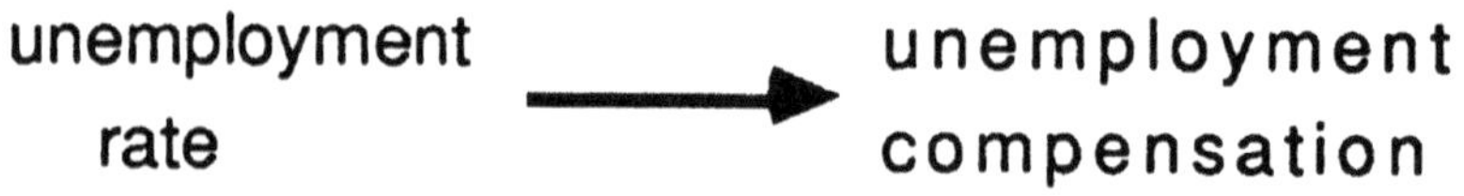

or the inflation rate is fed back to determine the money supply.

inflation rate → money supply

Thus the condition of the economy is fed back to determine the policy setting. So, for example, policy statements are not

> taxes should be cut

but rather

> taxes should be cut
>
> if
>
> unemployment is too high

Of course the actual rules that emerge from the use of the feedback framework are more complicated than the ones above and make the policy a function not just of one part of the economy but of many parts of the economy. For example, the tax-cut rule above would be a function not only of unemployment but also of inflation, the size of the deficit, and the balance of payments — but more on this later.

The feedback control framework not only provides results in the form of feedback rules but also provides bands or intervals for the outcomes. Thus the advice is not

Mr. President, if taxes are cut, then unemployment will drop to 6 percent.

But

Mr. President, if taxes are cut, then unemployment will drop to between 5 and 7 percent.

These bands or confidence intervals are a more realistic form of advice. In fact, economists cannot predict the future state of the economy with precision, and advice should be given that reflects this fact. The engineers who designed the moon lander did not say that it would land at some exact point. Rather they drew an oval on the map of the moon and said that there was a 90 percent probability that the moon lander would come to rest within the oval. Economies are even more subject to shocks, behavioral uncertainties, and measurement errors than are lunar landers. Therefore it is important that economists should adopt the same modest habits as their engineering colleagues. This occurs naturally in the feedback control framework because the results are presented not as points but as confidence intervals.

However, the greatest gains from the use of the feedback control framework may not come about from the employment of feedback rules or confidence intervals, but rather from common-sense changes in institutions and policy procedures that will come about once the economy is viewed through this framework. One example is the long decision lag in tax and expenditure policy. It now takes a year or more from the time unemployment rises until the President proposes and Congress passes changes in taxes or expenditures. Viewed through the framework of feedback control these long lags are intolerable and could be shortened considerably with some procedural changes on the part of Congress and the Administration. The job training programs periodically used to decrease unemployment are another example. Sometimes it takes so long to pass the legislation for these programs and to establish the institutional structures to administer them that by the time they go into effect inflation rather than unemployment is the main problem in the economy. A relatively minor change in the legislation could tie the expenditure levels on such programs in a feedback manner to the unemployment level so that expenditure rises immediately after the unemployment level rises.

So much for the gains from using the feedback framework. What are the problems with the use of the feedback framework? This approach, like any other has its limitations. The most important is the problem of establishing the goals. In fact there are two elements to the choice of goals — one of which is more difficult than the other. The first element is the selection of the targets or desired paths. Policymakers may not want to state explicitly their desired paths for the economy. They may prefer to leave such matters a little unclear. However, if they are willing to indicate desired paths, then the problem is to describe their hopes for unemployment, inflation, and growth rates, as well as for the size of the government deficit.

The second element — specifying the goals — is more difficult because it requires the assignment of relative weights to the several goals. For example, some presidents will care twice or three times as much about controlling inflation as about decreasing unemployment. Or the President may care more about inflation during the first two years of office but more about unemployment as the elections approach in the second two years in office. Policymakers may find it difficult to assign such weights. Engineers, however, have found ways to design automatic pilots that effectively keep an aircraft near its predetermined path; so it seems likely that economists and politicians can communicate about desired paths and weights so as to permit feedback policy systems to be designed with better performance than our present system provides.

A second limitation of feedback systems that has drawn much attention in the economics literature in recent years is behavioral responses to feedback rules. This idea is associated with the work on rational expectations. The reasoning is that airplanes and moon landers are inanimate objects that will not change their behavior when feedback rules are announced. However, if economists develop a feedback rule based on past behavior of individuals and announce the rule, then people will change their behavior in response to the announcement of the rule. For example, business executives change their prices periodically in a certain manner. However, if the Federal Reserve Board announces that it has developed a feedback rule for the money supply based on that behavior, then the executives may change their behavior. This may be a serious problem and the literature has treated it that way. Of course, the developer of the feedback rule may anticipate that individuals will change their behavior in response to the announcement of the rule. Then the original rule can be designed to take account of the expected change in behavior. In the same way, economic agents may anticipate that the designers of the rule will anticipate that . . . Thus a game may arise between the policymakers and the agents.

The importance of the response to the announcement of a feedback rule depends crucially on its magnitude and direction. Some economists think that the response will be in opposite directions from the policy and equal in magnitude to the policy with the result that the policy is completely offset. However, the majority of economists do not subscribe to this view. Some even argue that the response is so small that it can be ignored in most cases. In fact, we do not have much solid evidence about the magnitude of these responses and considerable empirical work must be done before the debate about magnitude and direction of response will be settled.

A third limitation of the feedback approach is the problem posed by the choice of model. For example, there is a continuing debate about whether changes in wealth cause changes in consumption. Thus there are two models — one that includes wealth in the consumption function and one that excludes wealth. If economists could run controlled laboratory experiments, this issue could be resolved, but such experiments cannot be run and we cannot be sure which is the correct model. This problem is not unique to the feedback framework. It is shared by all empirical approaches to macroeconomic policy determination.

A final limitation of the feedback approach is that lunar landers and airplanes have a single commander but economies do not. (Thermostats do not have a single commander either and we are all familiar with the problems this causes.) Not only the President but also Congress and the Federal Reserve Board play major roles in determining economic policy. The basic feedback framework does not take account of these sometimes conflicting roles. More advanced techniques in the feedback framework do attempt to take account of the roles of multiple decision makers. These techniques will be discussed later.

In summary, some of the limitations of the feedback control framework are

- the problem of choosing desired paths and weights
- responses to the announcements of feedback rules
- the problem of the correct choice of model
- multiple decision makers.

All these limitations will be discussed in detail in Part III.

At this point you may say, "Why should we use a framework that has all of these limitations?" The answer is that every framework for macroeconomic policy has major limitations. Moreover, it is not necessary to adopt a single framework when thinking about the economy. It is wiser to assess the strengths and weaknesses of each framework and to use each framework when and where it has a comparative advantage. The feedback control framework is useful for policy problems where there are desired paths that may be changing over time, where there are dynamic responses to policies, and where there is uncertainty.

The thesis of this book is that the feedback control framework offers a fresh approach to macroeconomic policy — an approach that will enable us to have a smoother economic life by damping the large swings in inflation and unemployment that have characterized the economy in recent years.

This book is divided into three parts. The first part discusses the components of the feedback framework. The second part describes policy results in the form of feedback rules. It also describes the use of confidence intervals and then discusses automatic stabilizers which work without explicit Congressional or Presidential action and which help to dampen fluctuations in the economy. The third section provides a detailed discussion of the limitations described above. The book closes with a discussion of the present status of macroeconomics and the feedback framework.

Before beginning the major sections of the book it is useful to review in the next chapter some of the past uses of feedback in macroeconomic policy.

2
Feedback: A Familiar Idea

Feedback is a familiar idea that has worked well in macroeconomic policy for fifty years under the name of automatic stabilizers. They are called *automatic* stabilizers because they go into effect without action by Congress or the Administration. Of these policies unemployment compensation is the most prominent but the stabilizing effect of income taxes is also well known. This chapter will discuss automatic stabilizers currently in use as well as a variety of other feedback policies that have been proposed but not passed into law.

1. Unemployment Compensation

The feedback effect of unemployment compensation is shown in Figure 2.1. At times businessmen decrease their investment out of concern that it will not be profitable. This in turn causes a decrease in the total income received by all consumers. The fall in income causes a decrease in purchases and a consequent increase in unemployment. The increase in unemployment then results in an increase in government spending to pay the unemployment compensation. Thus the change in unemployment feeds back to partially offset the original decline in investment.

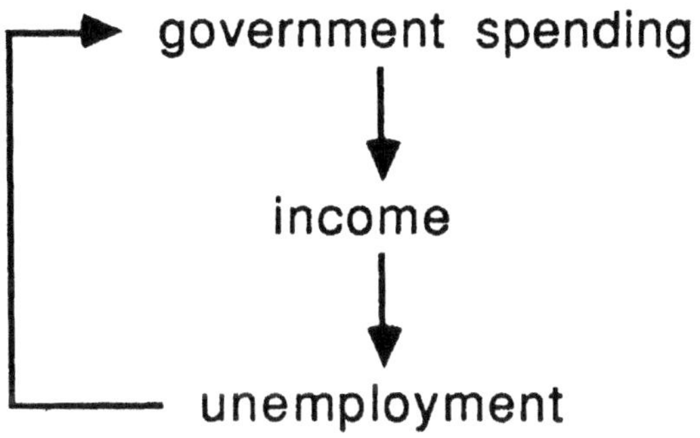

Figure 2.1. Feedback in Unemployment Compensation

Therefore unemployment compensation acts as an automatic stabilizer. It is automatic because Congress does not have to pass any legislation to cause the increase in unemployment compensation. It is stabilizing because the increase in unemployment compensation partially offsets the affects of the initial budget cuts and mitigates the increase in unemployment.

2. Income Taxes

When a recession occurs and income declines so do tax revenues. It is as though there is an automatic tax cut every time that a recession occurs. In fact, there is no decline in tax *rates* only in tax *revenues* as a consequence of the lower income levels. So there is no need for either Congress or the President to take any action. Tax revenues will decline when there is a recession. The government takes less out of the economy and there is a tendency toward stabilization.

In contrast to income taxes, real-estate taxes provide an example of taxes without stabilizing feedback. Since real-estates taxes do not vary from recession to expansion, no stabilization results from these taxes.

Both unemployment compensation and income taxes are examples of feedback policies that are in effect. Next consider several feedback ideas that policymakers have considered but decided not to use.

3. John F. Kennedy and the Small Tax Changes

The Council of Economic Advisers during the Kennedy Administration was Walter Heller (chairman), Kermit Gordon, and James Tobin. The staff of the Council included Robert Solow. These economists urged the President to propose to Congress that he be given authority to make small decreases in income taxes without Congressional approval. This would have decreased the time lag required to respond to a downturn. Kennedy made such a proposal but Congress did not act favorably on it. Talk of tax reduction was in the air at the time and Congress was determined that if taxes were to be cut it would be the one to do it.

This policy would not have been an automatic feedback policy but it would have decreased the time required for the President to implement a feedback action.

4. Inflation and the Federal Reserve Board

The Federal Reserve Board sometimes seems to operate on the feedback principle though its actions have nothing automatic about them. It watches the rate of inflation closely. When that rate begins to edge up the Board sometimes sells bonds so as to slow the rate of growth of the money supply and thus dampen the inflation.

5. Rostenkowski and the Reagan Tax Cuts

Congressman Dan Rostenkowski, chairman of the Ways and Means Committee, once proposed a feedback rule for tax changes. He suggested that the third year of the Reagan tax cuts should go into effect only if certain conditions were achieved in the economy. This is a variant of the proposal by John Kennedy, but in a form that is much more acceptable to Congress since it would not give the President authority to change taxes. In this case the tax change would be determined by the conditions in the economy and would not be delayed by long debates in either Congress or the Administration.

The above are feedback ideas that have been put into effect in the past or proposed on the common-sense notion that it is useful to lean against the wind, that is, when the economy is declining, measures are required to stimulate it. The rest of the book describes a framework for feedback control that includes the simple notion of leaning against the wind but provides a much more comprehensive view. This framework includes feedback rules that (1) depend not on a single condition like unemployment but on many conditions simultaneously, such as unemployment, inflation, growth, and the balance of payments; (2) include consideration for the length of lags in many different parts of the economy; and (3) include consideration of the sources and types of uncertainty in the economy.

Part I
Feedback: A New Framework

As was described in the previous chapter feedback is a familiar idea in economics. The extension of this idea to include policy rules that depend not just on a single indicator but on many indicators and that encompass dynamics and uncertainty offers a new approach to macroeconomic policy determination. In order to understand this approach, an encompassing view of the feedback framework is needed. To this end the three aspects of the feedback framework (goals, dynamics, and uncertainty) will be discussed in the following chapters.

3
Goals

Goals for economic policy are normally stated as "4 percent unemployment" or "a balanced budget." They do not include any indication of timing. However, there is usually an implicit understanding of time so that the goal for unemployment may be "to reduce unemployment from 8 percent to 6 percent in the first year of the Administration and to 4 percent in the second year." Then the goal becomes a desired path for the unemployment rate. Similarly, most presidents do not talk about balancing the budget in the first year of their administration but rather about reducing it gradually until it is balanced in the last year of the administration. Here again the goal is a desired path. This chapter on goals in dynamic systems is thus really a chapter on desired paths for a few key economic variables like unemployment, inflation, the deficit, and government spending.

The specification of the desired paths alone, however, is not sufficient to describe the goals in the feedback framework. Rather, since the desired paths for various indicators such as unemployment and inflation may be conflicting, it is also necessary to assign weights or priorities to the various desired paths. Thus, if it is more important to reduce unemployment than to reduce the deficit, then a high weight is assigned to unemployment and a low weight to the deficit. The discussion of these weights constitutes the second section in this chapter.

1. Desired Paths

The most insightful way to discuss desired paths is to examine the actual path followed by the economy in recent years. This provides a perspective on the political and economic events that affect both desired and actual paths for the economy.

A list of desired paths for the economy — both indicators of the state of the economy and policy variables — would include these at least:

- unemployment rate
- inflation rate
- balance of payments
- government deficit
- GNP growth rates
- income distribution
- government spending
- tax rates
- interest rates.

However, it would make this chapter much too long to discuss desired paths for all of these indicators, so four will be singled out for discussion here, namely, unemployment, inflation, the deficit, and government expenditures. It should be emphasized that the other indicators are not left out of feedback models — indeed they are a key part of many of these models.

Ch. 3. Goals

a. Unemployment Rate

First consider the unemployment rates in the post-World War II period as plotted in Figure 3.1. The lowest unemployment rates were during the Korean and Vietnam wars when the rate went below 4 percent. The highest unemployment rate was above 10 percent and was reached during Reagan's first term after he cut back many government programs. Another peak in the unemployment rate occurred in 1974 after the OPEC oil embargo when the rate soared to about 9 percent.

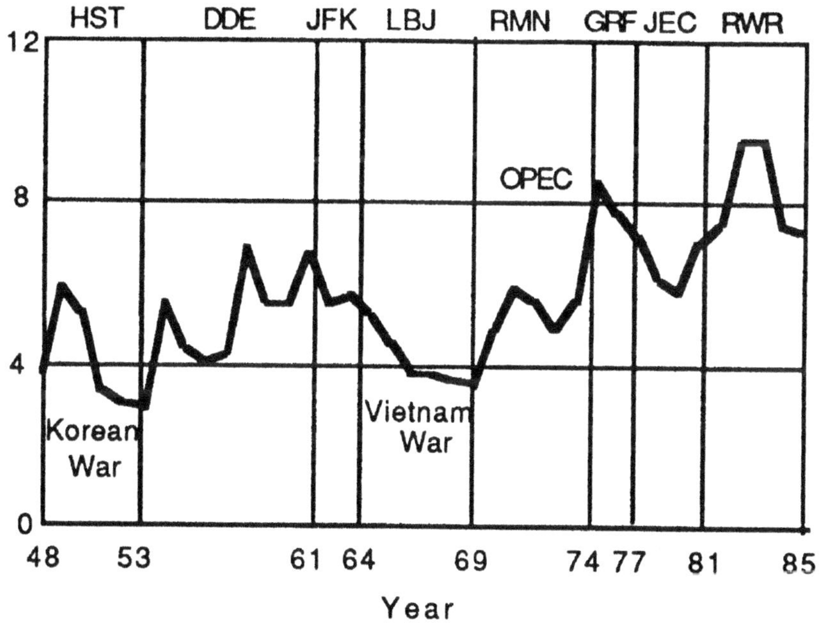

Figure 3.1. Unemployment Rate in Percent, 1948-85

What then is a reasonable goal for unemployment? Until the seventies the commonly discussed goal was 4 percent. However, in the last ten years we have experienced so much unemployment that in the minds of many the goal has drifted upward to 5 or 6 percent.

The desired path for unemployment during an administration would thus normally be to reduce the unemployment rate from its initial level in steps to 4 or 5 percent. For example, the unemployment rate when Reagan entered office was about 8 percent. His desired path might have been to reduce unemployment by 2 percent in each of his first two years and then to hold it constant at 4 percent.

Consider next the other primary concern of most presidents, namely, controlling the inflation rate.

b. Inflation Rate

The inflation rate is considerably more volatile than the unemployment rate; however, the big peaks and valleys are still clear as is shown in Figure 3.2.

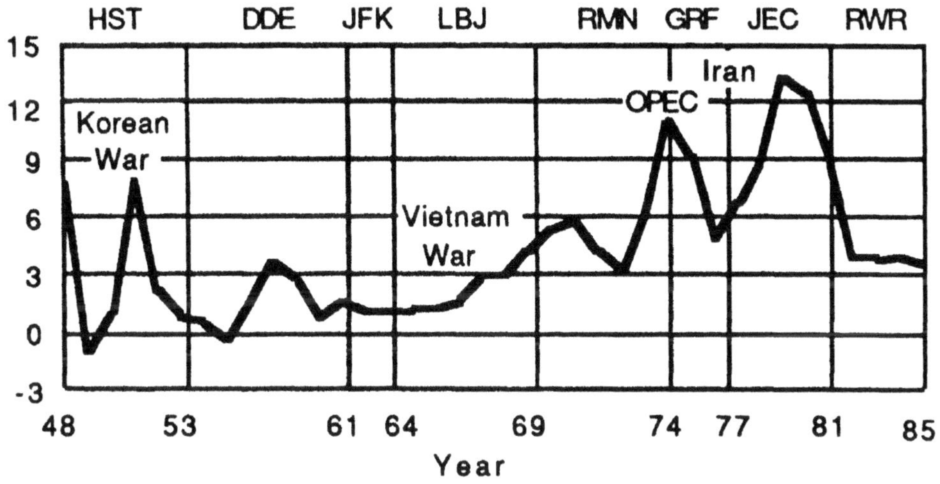

Figure 3.2. Inflation Rate in Percent, 1948-85

The inflation rate reached one of its highs during the Korean War. After that the other two periods of very high inflation were the 11 percent rate after the OPEC oil embargo in 1973 and the 14 percent rate that resulted from the Iranian oil crisis in 1979. By comparison to these three periods, the inflation during the Vietnam War looks mild indeed. Also prominent in the chart is the dramatic decline in the inflation rate during Reagan's first term in office.

Now what about the desired inflation rate? For most people constant prices or a zero inflation rate is desirable. On second thought many people would say that they preferred a low inflation rate of a few percentage points — one that is consistent with an unemployment rate of 4, 5, or 6 percent. However, when choosing goals in the feedback framework one does not have to select a consistent set. Thus one can choose an unemployment rate of 4 percent and an inflation rate of 0 percent, knowing that they cannot both be achieved.

The desired path for inflation in an administration is usually a slow decrease in the inflation rate from its initial level to a rate of a few percentage points just before the next Presidential election. For example, when Reagan began his first term the inflation rate was 10 percent. His goal might have been to have the inflation rate drop by 2 percentage points each year so that it was only 2 percent by the time he was running for re-election in 1984.

c. Government Expenditures

Inflation and unemployment occupy center stage but they do not stand alone as goals for the economy. The rate of growth of government expenditures is also a key goal.

Many voters in the 1980 election wanted to see a decrease in the size of the federal government. Thus their desired path for government expenditures would have been a sharp — or a least a slow — decline in federal government expenditures. Ronald Reagan, however, did not say that he planned to decrease government expenditures but rather that he planned to decrease the rate of growth of government expenditures. A quick glance at Figure 3.3 shows that a major part of government expenditures, government purchases of goods and services, followed a jagged path during Reagan's first term but that the overall direction was up.

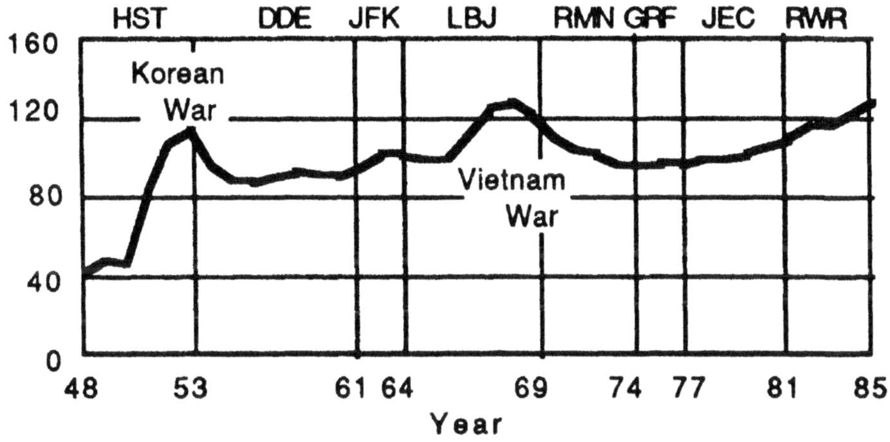

Figure 3.3. Federal Government Purchases in 1972 Dollars

Except for the increases during the Korean and Vietnam wars government purchases of goods and services have grown little until the recent increase in defense expenditures that began in the Carter Administration and extends into the Reagan Administration.

Next consider the desired path. It is apparent that the desired path for government purchases may differ strongly from President to President. Some will prefer a slow growth in these expenditures, some will want a slow decline and some will prefer continued growth but at a slower rate. Of course, these preferences have implications for government expenditure growth and consequently for the government deficit, as is discussed next.

d. The Government Deficit

A quick glance at Figure 3.4 shows the large size of the government deficit in the Reagan Administration - even when deflated and plotted in terms of 1967 dollars.

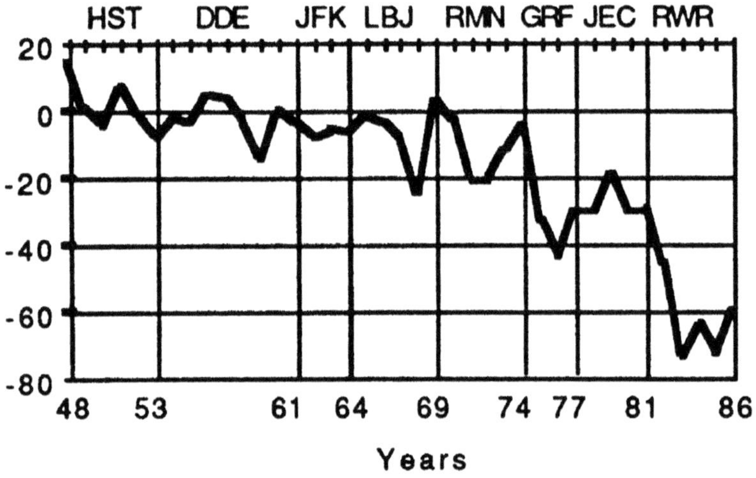

Figure 3.4. Deficit in Billions of 1967 Dollars

Now what about goals for the deficit? Many presidents announce that they will balance the budget by the end of their term in office. So the desired path is a decrease in the deficit in each year until a zero deficit is achieved in the year of the next election. Interestingly enough, Figure 3.4 shows that Truman, Eisenhower, Kennedy, Johnson, and Nixon were not so far away from the goal of zero deficit at the end of their terms in office but Ford, Carter, and Reagan missed the goal substantially.

In summary, most presidents favor desired paths that reduce unemployment, inflation, and the deficit. In contrast, presidents differ sharply about desired paths for government expenditures.

Presidents will also have announced or unannounced desired paths for tax rates, the balance of payments, GNP growth rates, income distribution, and interest rates. The feedback framework permits the specification of desired paths for all of these indicators of the economy's performance. The desired paths need not be consistent — as is true of the desired paths of most presidents — they need only be desired. However, it is necessary in the feedback framework to specify weights for each path to indicate their relative importance to the President.

2. Weights

Desired paths — that is a reasonable notion — but weights! How is one going to ask a President to specify weights or priorities that indicate the relative importance he or she attaches to inflation and unemployment? Most presidents would probably have some relative weights in the back of their minds but to express them in hard fixed numbers — that is difficult.

For some insight into this problem one can look at the problem of weight selection in engineering design problems where feedback control methods have been used with great success. Consider, for example, the design of an automatic pilot for a large commercial aircraft like the giant Boeing 747. The desired path for the plane is a nice smooth flight path. Also, there are desired paths for controls like the stick and the rudder pedals. These desired paths for controls specify that they should not be moved so suddenly as to jerk the passengers around.

In the design of an automatic pilot it is necessary to assign weights both to the aircraft path and to the paths for movements of the controls. If one assigns high weights to the aircraft path and low weights to the control paths, the automatic pilot will respond to a sudden gust of wind by sharply jerking the plane back onto the desired path. This will cause substantial discomfort to the passengers as the contents of coffee cups and cocktail glasses are splashed around the passenger cabin. But if one assigns low weights to the plane's path and high weights to the paths for the controls, then the automatic pilot will gently guide the plane back onto the desired path so smoothly that the passengers will hardly notice. This is just fine when the airplane is at 40,000 feet but is less desirable when the aircraft is landing. During the landing any deviations from the desired path must be corrected quickly or the discomfort to the passengers will be more dire than spilled coffee.

Thus the relative weights are important. However, if you were to ask an aeronautical engineer to assign weights to the plane's path and to the control paths he or she would be at just as great a loss as a President trying to assign relative weights to inflation and unemployment. If this is so then how are the relative weights assigned in the automatic-pilot design problem?

The answer is simple. They are chosen by trial and error until the desired trade–off is attained. This is not done in the aircraft but in computer simulations of the flight of the aircraft.

A similar procedure can be used in macroeconomic systems. An initial set of weights can be assigned and the resulting policies can be analyzed with computer simulations to see if the economy is jerked back on to its course too suddenly or is allowed to remain off course for too long. Then the relative weights can be adjusted.

One can also ask if the weights will vary over time. The answer is a definite yes. Most presidents are quite willing to have the economy be off course during the first two or three years of their administration but are concerned that it be on course in the months preceding the Presidential election. Thus the weights may be relatively small early in the term and progressively larger as the Presidential election approaches.

Also, the weights may change with developments in the economy. For example, when balance-of-payments problems persist over long periods of time, decreasing the imbalance begins to play a large role in the political process and the weight attached to this balance would be increased.

3. Summary

In summary, the feedback framework requires that the President be able to select desired paths for key indicators of the economy's performance and to assign relative weights to these paths. Desired paths are a familiar notion in the political economy of macroeconomics but weights are not. However, computer simulations can be used to choose the weights so that the resulting feedback rules can be used to guide the economy along the desired paths with a minimum of discomfort.

4
Dynamics

"The data which we will release to the press tomorrow show that unemployment rose by three–tenths of a percent last month." This cryptic sentence in a report from the Labor Department to the White House is the first notice that a downturn may be occurring in the economy. How long will it take for the government to decide to take action to stem the rise in unemployment? Then how long will it take for the economy to respond to the government's initiative so that unemployment declines again?

A long time.

A long time indeed. First, it takes the government many months to decide to act — the decision lag. Then it takes consumers and producers additional months to respond to the government's initiative — the effect lag. This chapter begins with sections on the decision and effect lags. Then in the last part of the chapter the economic models that embody these dynamics are described.

1. Decision Lags

The cryptic message above is received first by the Council of Economic Advisers and the Treasury. They pass it along to the President but do not propose immediate action because "one swallow does not make it summer". The economy may improve next month on its own without any help from the government.

If, however, unemployment continues to rise for several months the Council and the Treasury may recommend to the President that he take action by proposing a cut in taxes. Legislation is drafted in the Treasury and duly sent to Capitol Hill.

Hearings on the legislation are scheduled by the House Ways and Means Committee. After the hearings the Committee makes some modification in the legislation and sends it to the House of Representatives for action. The House debates and passes the bill and sends it to the Senate, where the process is repeated. Finally, compromises on the differences between the House and Senate versions are reached and a final bill is passed by both houses and sent to the President for his signature. The President quickly signs the bill and orders the Treasury to implement the tax cut. The Treasury issues the appropriate regulations and tax withholding is decreased the next month.

How long did all that take? How long is the decision lag — the time from the first increase in unemployment until the consumer looks at his paycheck and realizes that he has more money to spend that month? Just about a year.

If the first increase in unemployment occurs in October the calendar of events might be as follows:

October	first increase in unemployment
November	continued increase in unemployment

December	continued increase in unemployment President asks the Treasury to prepare legislation
January	legislation sent to Congress
February	hearings in the House Ways and Means Committee
March	Committee action
April	passage by the House of Representatives
May - July	Senate hearings and passage
August	conference committee action and final passage
September	Presidential signature and Treasury action

A full year to decide on a course of action to combat the rise in unemployment!

But what about monetary policy? Admittedly fiscal policy with its changes in taxes and expenditures by Congress has a long decision lag — but what about monetary policy changes? Surely the Federal Reserve Board can make decisions more quickly than the President and Congress.

Right, the Federal Reserve Board meets frequently and does not need Congressional approval to act. Therefore the decision lag for changes in the money supply is short — only a matter of a few months. However, the effect lag on monetary policy can be very long.

2. Effect Lags

The Federal Reserve Board decides to increase the money supply in order to decrease unemployment. How long does it take for this policy to take effect?

A decision is made in the morning to increase the money supply. That afternoon bonds are bought on the New York bond market to begin the increase in the money supply. The effective interest rate on Treasury bills drops within minutes and other interest rates follow along in the next few days and weeks. This is fast but the next step is slower. The decrease in interest rates causes consumers to purchase more automobiles since it is now cheaper and easier to borrow the money to buy a car. Also, the lower interest rates may entice more people into buying new homes. Here, however, the lag is longer still — maybe six months to a year. Finally, the lower interest rates may cause firms to purchase more new machines and build new factories. But here the lag is very long — a year and a half to two years.

So the effect lag in monetary policy is mixed. Some parts, like automobile purchases, have short lags of a few months and other parts, like equipment purchases and plant construction, have long lags of a year or two.

What about the effect lag of fiscal policy changes like decreases in taxes or increases in government expenditures? These too are mixed depending on the particular policy used. If taxes are decreased, consumers respond by increasing expenditures within a matter of months. If expenditures are increased, the lag may be longer while new government programs are set up or existing programs expanded.

The decision and effect lags can then be summarized in Table 4.1, which shows the number of months associated with each lag.

Table 4.1.
Decision and Effect Lags for Fiscal and Monetary Policy

	Lag (months)		
	Decision	Effect	Total
Fiscal	12	3	15
Monetary	2	10	12

As the totals indicate, neither monetary nor fiscal policy can respond quickly to increases in unemployment.

Of course there is considerable uncertainty about the exact lengths of these lags. However, there is no uncertainty about the fact that the lags exist and that they result in a dynamic response in our macroeconomics system. Methods of making effective policy in the face of these lags will be discussed later. First it is necessary to show how these lags are represented in economic models.

3. Lags in Economic Models

The lags in economic models are represented by equations. For example, the effect of interest rates on investment in new equipment can be represented by

interest rates in month t	---->	investment in month t plus 14.

That is, changes in interest rates cause a change in investment fourteen months later. For example, the rate of interest in January of one year is low enough to entice an entrepreneur into deciding to expand her production facilities. However, it takes fourteen months to draw up the plans, let the bids and begin the construction. The investment expenditure in March of one year is thus affected by interest rates in January of the previous year.

Another example is the effect of tax changes on the purchase of automobiles. This is modeled with two equations. The first equation is

income minus taxes = disposable income.

The income that you can dispose of is the amount you receive less the taxes you pay. The second equation then relates disposable income to automobile purchases

disposable income in month t	--->	automobile purchases in month t plus 3.

When taxes fall and your disposable income is increased you may decide to use the extra money in your checking account to buy a new car. However, it takes you three months to select the car, arrange a loan and receive delivery.

Economic models are constructed from equations of this sort. A complete model may have from fifty to three hundred equations that model the dynamic response of the economy to a dozen different policy variables, such as tax rates, expenditure levels, and the amount of money in circulation. These models are a central part of the feedback method.

The models contain two types of variables

- state variables
- control variables

State variables describe the state of the economy but cannot be *directly* modified by policymakers. Some examples of state variables are

- unemployment rate
- inflation rate
- gross national product
- exports
- imports.

In contrast, control variables are variables that can be directly controlled by policymakers, such as

- income tax rates
- government expenditures
- open market operations to affect the money supply.

So in the feedback framework control variables are used to affect the state variables in order to guide the economy along desired paths.

4. Summary

The lags in economic policy are of two types — decision lags and effect lags. These lags cause the economy to respond over time to policy changes and thus to be a dynamic system. That system can be represented with an economic model with state variables and control variables.

This chapter gives the impression that everything is cut and dried. Unemployment increases and after so many months a policy change takes effect and after so many more months consumers respond to the policy change. Not so! Economists do not know exactly how long it will take the President and the Congress to make a decision. Neither do we know exactly how long it will take for consumers to respond to a tax cut. Nor do we know exactly how much of the tax cut they will spend and how much they will save. Indeed there is much uncertainty in the economy. Some methods of economic analysis ignore this uncertainty. However, feedback methods are designed to accommodate uncertainty, which is the subject of the next chapter.

5
Uncertainty

Uncertainty is pervasive in macroeconomics. One need only look at the forecasting records of the most talented analysts or of the most sophisticated computer models to realize the amount of uncertainty in the economy. Yet most methods of macroeconomic policy determination ignore uncertainty. In contrast, feedback methods incorporate uncertainty fully into the analysis of policy options.

Of course, one response to the sentences above is, "So what! No method of analysis will eliminate the uncertainty, so why bother using a method that takes it into account." The answer is that there are different degrees of uncertainty associated with different policies. While in the end the President may not always choose to employ the policy with the least uncertainty, he would like to be able to make an informed judgment.

There may be two routes over the mountain. One is quick but dangerous and the other is slow but safe. On some days you may choose the dangerous route and on other days the safe route. However, you want to know which route is dangerous and which is safe and from that knowledge to make an informed choice. Worst of all, you do not want to choose the dangerous route without knowing its risk only to discover the truth when you are high in the mountains. So it is with macroeconomic policy. Some policies may be sure but slow and others may be fraught with uncertainty but fast. For example, fiscal policy with its long decision lag as it proceeds through the President and Congress may be slow but sure. Monetary policy, on the other hand, will be quicker because it has a shorter decision lag, but since the response of the economy to changes in interest rates cannot be predicted with great precision, it is more uncertain.

However, uncertainty occurs not only in the response to policy. Rather there are various kinds of uncertainty. In fact there are three kinds of uncertainty that are distinguished in the feedback framework:

- shock
- behavioral
- measurement.

An example of shock uncertainty is the shock that was caused by the OPEC oil embargo in 1973. Another shock was the failure of the Russian wheat crop in 1973 with its large impact on world wheat prices. Such shocks are not a response within the macroeconomic system under analysis but are external to it. On the other hand, behavioral uncertainty is the uncertain response to a policy. When taxes are cut consumers spend more; however, economists do not know exactly how much of the additional take-home income will be spent and how much will be saved. In response to one tax cut consumers may spend 95 percent of their additional income and save only 5 percent. In response to the next tax cut consumers may spend 85 percent of their additional income and save 15 percent. Finally, measurement uncertainty is related to knowing where we are. Economic statistics provide a description of the state of the economy, but there is uncertainty in these measurements — more uncertainty in some measurements than in others. For example, consumption data are relatively accurate while inventory investment data are much more uncertain since they are based on the change in the stocks of inventories.

1. Shock Uncertainty

When OPEC began the oil embargo in 1973 a shock wave flashed through the world economy. Oil prices went up immediately followed by all energy prices in the ensuing months. Then food and other prices rose within the year in response to the increased cost of production. As consumers chose smaller European and Japanese models, automobile workers in Detroit were laid off.

About the same time the Russian wheat crop failed and that government made large purchases of wheat on the international markets. The quick rise in wheat prices was followed by an increase in the prices of many other types of food. This in turn caused balance-of-payments problems for many poor countries that were large importers of food.

Shocks are thus external to the economic systems under analysis. That is, the failure of the Russian wheat crop is outside of the U.S. macroeconomic system. Similarly, the world oil price is largely determined by forces outside of the U.S. economy. Also, from a European perspective policy actions taken by U.S. officials are viewed as shocks.

2. Behavioral Uncertainty

The government cuts taxes. Consumers have more money to spend. Some of the money will be saved and some will be spent. The behavior of consumers cannot be predicted perfectly. Rather we know that on average consumers will save 10 percent of the increased income and spend 90 percent of it. However, in response to a given tax cut the proportion spent may be higher or lower than 90 percent. Yet most methods of macroeconomic analysis treat the percentage spent as though it were known exactly. The bar graph in Figure 5.1 illustrates this.

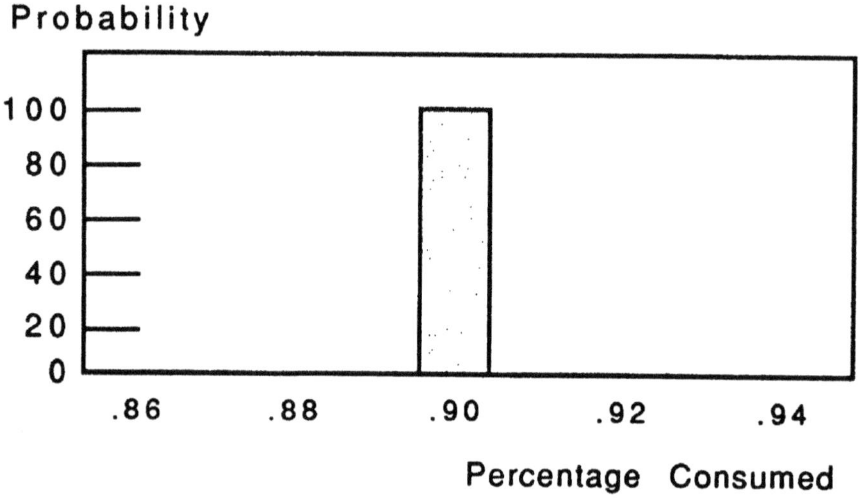

Figure 5.1. Certainty about the Percentage Consumed

The percentage of the tax cut that will be consumed is plotted along the horizontal axis. The probability that consumers will consume each percentage is plotted on the vertical axis. Thus Figure 5.1 indicates that there is a 100 percent probability that .90 of the additional income will be consumed. In contrast in Figure 5.2 there is a 20 percent probability that .88 will be consumed, a 60 percent probability that .90 will be consumed and a 20 percent probability that .92 will be consumed.

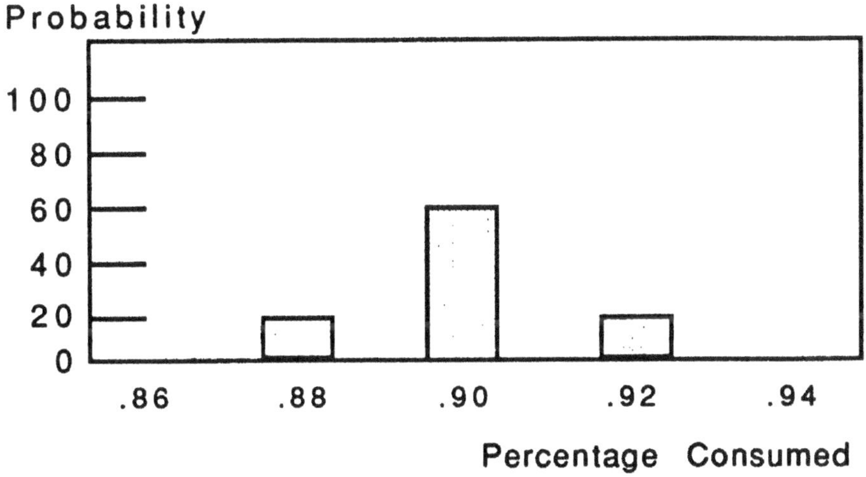

Figure 5.2. Uncertainty about the Percentage Consumed

Thus the economist who uses Figure 5.2 rather than Figure 5.1 is a little more modest (or realistic) about what he knows. The first economist says "Mr. President, if you give the American people a tax cut, they will spend nine-tenths of it." The second economist says "Mr. President, if you give the American people a tax cut, they will spend between .88 and .92 of it."

In fact the uncertainty about the behavioral response

may be even greater as shown in Figure 5.3. Now the range is from .86 to .94 and smaller probabilities are assigned to each level.

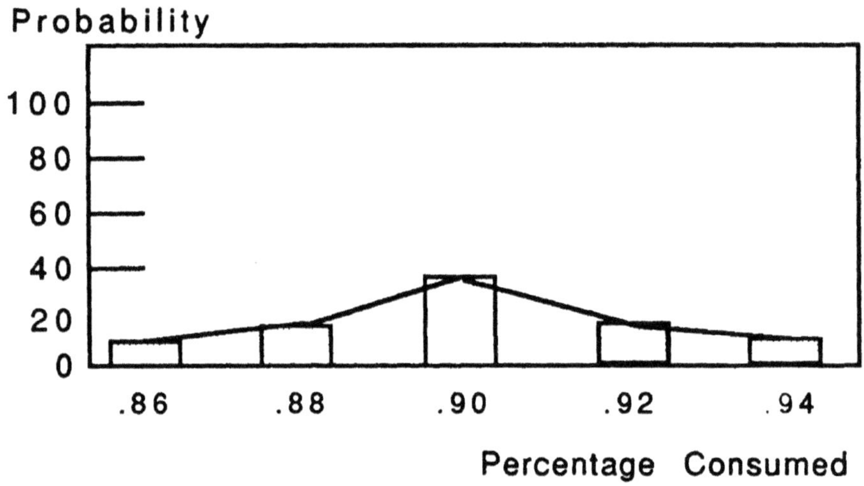

Figure 5.3. More Uncertainty about the Percentage Consumed

Also a line has been drawn between the tops of the bars in the bar graph in Figure 5.3. As the number of discrete levels is increased from three in Figure 5.2 to five in Figure 5.3 to nine in Figure 5.4 this line becomes a smooth curve.

The smooth curve in Figure 5.4 is a probability distribution that can be used to describe an uncertain behavioral response. In fact when economic models are estimated with statistical methods by fitting lines and curves to the historical data, one of the by-products of the estimation process is a distribution like that shown in

Figure 5.4. However, for most methods of macroeconomic policy determination the distribution is thrown away and only the central value of .9 is used. This gives a false sense of security

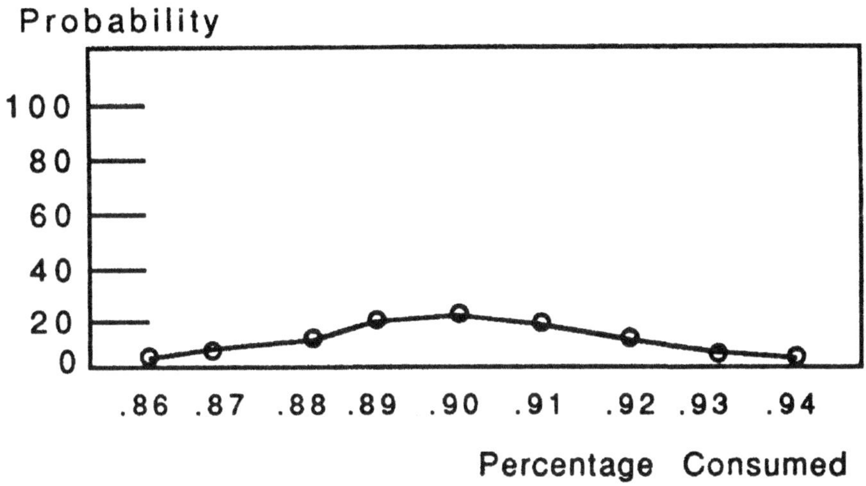

Figure 5.4. Nine Levels Plotted as a Smooth Curve

to policymakers — security that quickly vanishes as time passes and the predicted values are not realized. Then the economic models are discredited. In contrast the feedback method carries the uncertainty through the analysis and promises less exact results.

One way this uncertainty is communicated is with the use of *confidence intervals*. These intervals are used to make statements like "I am 40 percent confident that the percentage consumed will be between .89 and .91." The basis for this kind of a statement is shown in Figure 5.5,

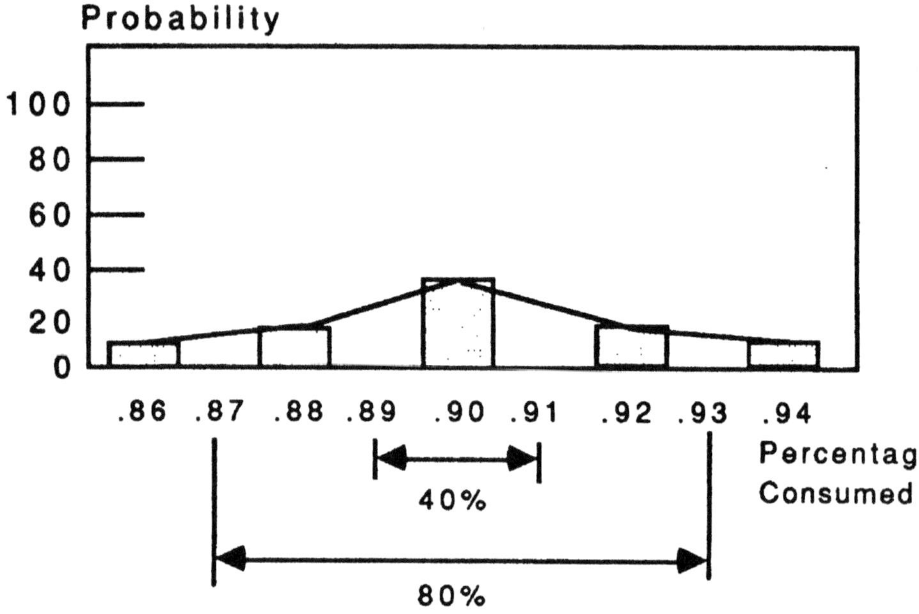

Figure 5.5. The Development of Confidence Intervals

which is Figure 5.3 with a few additions. There is a 40 percent probability that the percentage consumed will be between .89 and .91 and an 80 percent probability that the percentage consumed will be between .87 and .93. The way the 80 percent probability is determined is shown in Table 5.1.

Table 5.1.
Determination of Probability of Percentage Consumed

Percentage Consumed	Probability
.88	20
.90	40
.92	20
Total	80

Thus as the interval widens the probability that the percentage consumed falls in the interval increases.

However, confidence intervals are not usually displayed as horizontal lines as in Figure 5.5 but as vertical lines as in Figure 5.6

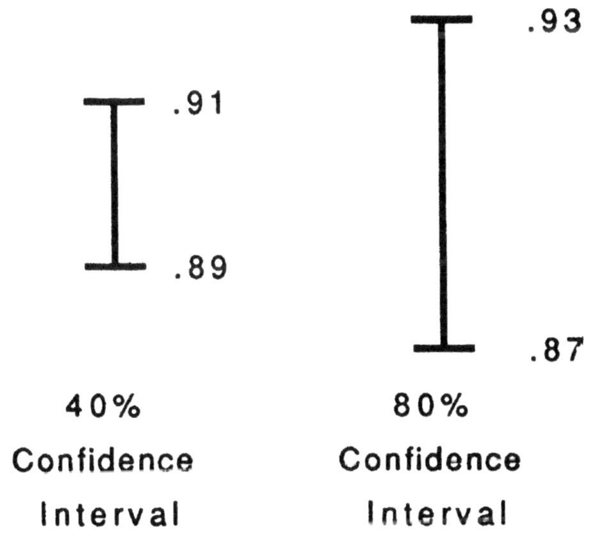

Figure 5.6. Confidence Intervals

This confidence interval would then be the basis for the statement, "Ms. President, I do not know exactly what percentage of the tax cut will be spent but I am 80 percent certain that it will be between .87 and .93."

Of course the President will not really care about the confidence interval for the percentage consumed - but she may be deeply interested in the confidence interval for unemployment. The form of this statement would be "Ms. President, if you cut taxes by 5 percent in November, then I am 80 percent certain that the unemployment rate in September just before the election will be between 7.5 percent and 8.5 percent."

The calculations that underlie such statements are too long and complicated for this book but the first step in such calculations can be easily illustrated. That step would be the calculation of the amount of consumption. If after-tax income were two trillion dollars the consumption could be calculated as

$$\textit{consumption} = \textit{(percentage consumed) (after-tax income)}.$$

The bottom end of the 80% confidence interval would be

$$\textit{1.74 trillion dollars} = \textit{(.87)(2 trillion dollars)}$$

and the top end would be

$$\textit{1.86 trillion dollars} = \textit{(.93)(2 trillion dollars)}.$$

The 80 percent confidence interval for consumption would thus be as shown in Figure 5.7.

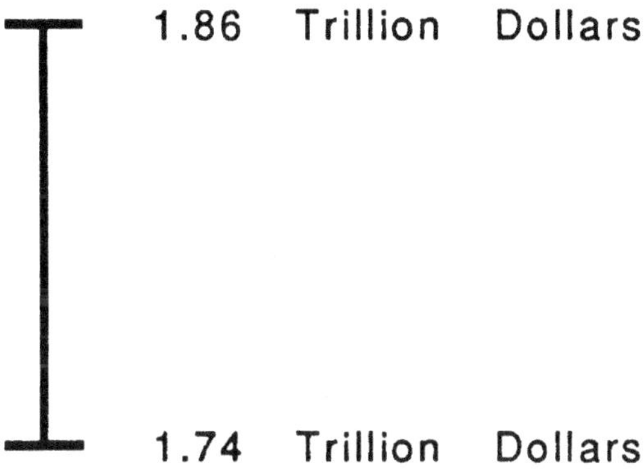

Figure 5.7. Confidence Interval for Consumption

So a confidence interval for the percentage consumed translates into a confidence interval for consumption. Then in a number of steps this translates into a confidence interval for unemployment.

Thus the behavioral uncertainty about the response to a tax cut gives rise to the necessity to provide the President with a confidence interval for unemployment rather than a single point prediction. For some policies these confidence intervals may be rather narrow and for other policies they may be extremely wide. For example, the relative confidence intervals for consumption responses to tax cuts and for investment responses to interest rate changes might be as shown below in Figure 5.8.

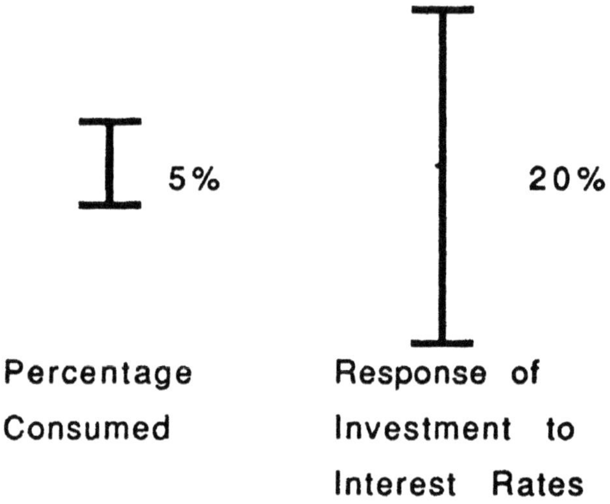

Figure 5.8. Relative Confidence Intervals for Behavioral Responses

The 80 percent confidence interval for percentage consumed might be from .88 to .92, that is a range of about 5 percent. In contrast the 80 percent confidence interval for the response of investment to interest rates would be a range of 20 percent of the value of the response.

The behavioral response of consumers to tax changes would be more certain than the response of producers to interest rate changes. Thus fiscal policy working through tax cuts would produce a narrower confidence interval than monetary policy working through interest rate changes. Therefore the confidence interval for unemployment would be much narrower when fiscal policy is used than when monetary policy is used.

3. Measurement Uncertainty

The usual assumption in macroeconomic policy analysis is that we know exactly where we are. Thus it is assumed that the are no errors in our economic data. Unfortunately, this is not true. Moreover, some measurements include larger errors than others. For example, if consumption data were subject to smaller measurement errors than inventory investment then the confidence intervals for these two measurements might be as shown below in Figure 5.9. In this situation policymakers would know to place less trust in inventory investment data than in consumption data. The feedback approach fully incorporates measurement errors into the analysis. Thus those data which are known to have large measurement errors are not relied on as heavily as those data with smaller measurement errors.

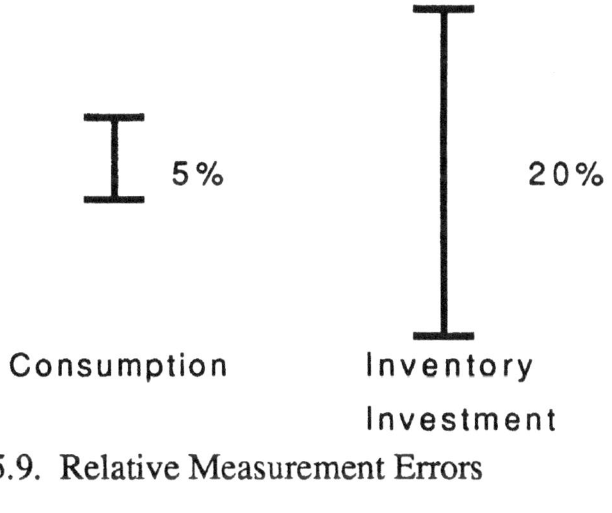

Figure 5.9. Relative Measurement Errors

Feedback

This concludes the discussion of uncertainty and completes the description of the elements of the feedback framework. These elements can be used to develop macroeconomic policy as is discussed in the Part II.

Part II
Policy in a Feedback Framework

The discussion of policy in this part of the book begins with a detailed discussion of feedback rules. Then uncertainty is introduced again and confidence intervals are discussed in the context of policy. This part then closes with a return to automatic stabilizers but now with the feedback framework in mind.

6
Feedback Rules

A simple feedback rule determines the level of taxes by "feeding back" the current level of unemployment. The rule indicates that taxes should be cut if unemployment is too high. More-complicated feedback rules make the tax rate a function of the levels of both unemployment and inflation. Still more realistic rules determine the level of both taxes and government expenditure simultaneously from the levels of unemployment and inflation.

1. Simple Feedback Rules

Figure 6.1 shows the structure of a simple feedback rule. Tax rates affect the economy to determine the unemployment rate.

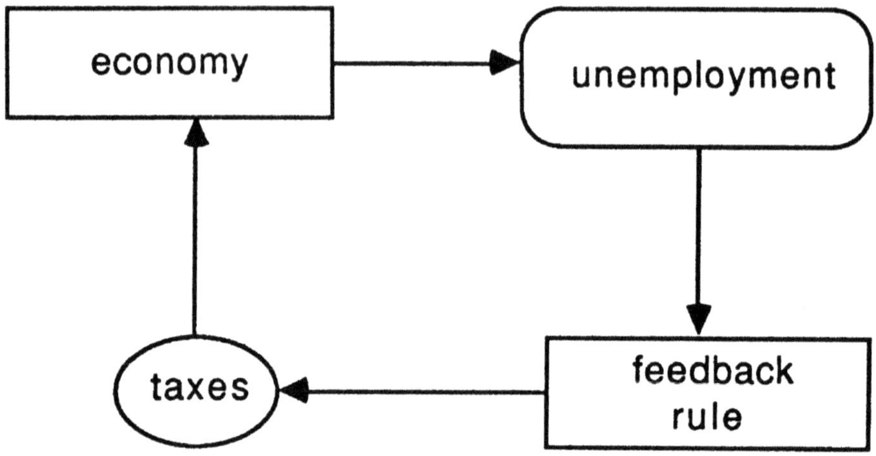

Figure 6.1. A Simple Feedback Rule

Then unemployment in the current quarter is "fed back" to determine the level of taxes for the next quarter. If unemployment is too high the feedback rule indicates that taxes should be cut so as to stimulate the economy. If unemployment is too low the feedback rule indicates that taxes should be increased so as to decrease the level of economic activity.

Current economic policy does not work this way. Instead problems in the economy build up over long periods of time while the President and Congress deliberate about what is the best action. Eventually a new level of taxes is set, but by the time a decision is finally reached much needless suffering has occurred.

A simple feedback rule that can be used for the money supply is shown in Figure 6.2. If unemployment is too

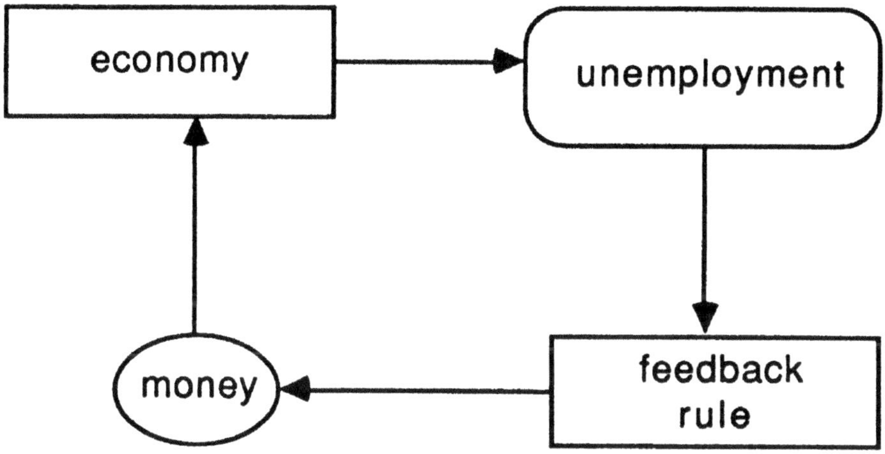

Figure 6.2. A Simple Feedback Rule for the Money Supply

high, the rate of growth of the money stock is increased in order to lower interest rates and stimulate the economy. If unemployment rates are too low the rate of growth of the money stock is decreased in order to raise interest rates and slow the growth of the economy.

2. More Complex Feedback Rules

The simple rules above ignore the fact that tax changes affect both inflation and unemployment. However, morc complex feedback rules take this into account as is shown in Figure 6.3.

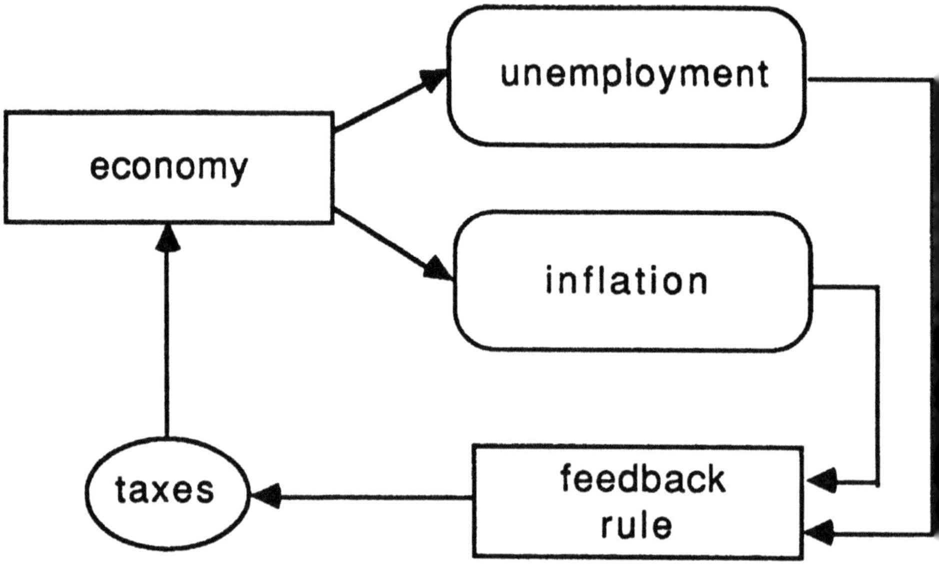

Figure 6.3. Feedback of Both Unemployment and Inflation

If unemployment is too high and inflation is moderate, then the feedback rule will indicate that taxes should be cut. However, if inflation is high the feedback rule will not indicate a tax cut even if unemployment is high. The feedback rule thus strikes a balance between inflation and unemployment. That balance is determined in part by the weights that are assigned to inflation and unemployment when setting the goals for the economy (as was discussed in Chapter 3).

More complex feedback rules determine both taxes and the money stock by feeding back both unemployment and inflation as shown in Figure 6.4. If unemployment is high and inflation is low, then the feedback rule will indicate

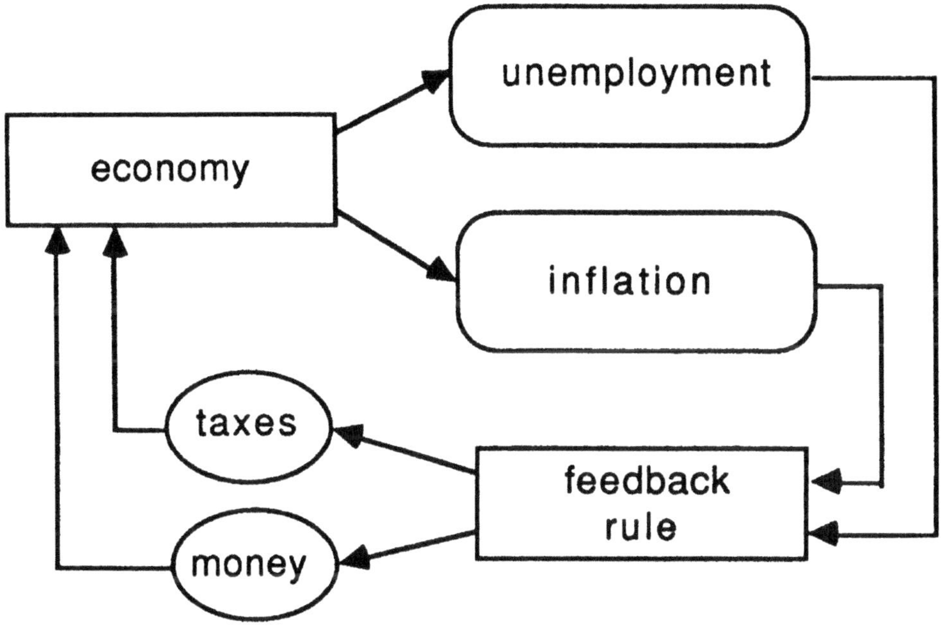

Figure 6.4. Taxes and Money in a Feedback Rule

the combined use of taxes and the money supply to lower unemployment without producing too much inflation. When both taxes and the money supply are included in the feedback rule the comparative advantage of each policy can be used. For example, since monetary policy may work more quickly than fiscal policy, it might be used first. However, monetary policy has the drawback that its effects are narrow; it hits a few sectors like automobiles and housing very hard because interest rate changes have their greatest effects on these sectors. In contrast, changes in taxes have a much more diffuse effect over the entire economy. So monetary policy might be used as a first check on the rise in unemployment followed by fiscal policy.

Also, if there is a difference in the uncertainty associated with monetary and fiscal policy, the feedback rule reflects these differences. For example, because of the great uncertainty in the effect of interest rates on plant and equipment investment, monetary policy may be a more uncertain instrument than tax changes. Then the feedback rule would place relatively less reliance on monetary policy.

One additional aspect of feedback rules is important. Under simple feedback rules, taxes in the winter are determined by unemployment in the fall. Policies in each quarter are thus determined by the condition of the economy in the previous quarter. However, for adequate stabilization it is usually necessary that the policy be determined by the condition of the economy in several previous quarters.

3. Feedback Rules with Multiple Lags

Figure 6.5 shows a feedback rule in which taxes and money in the winter are determined by unemployment in the fall and by inflation in the previous spring, summer, and fall. Why are feedback rules with these multiple lags necessary?

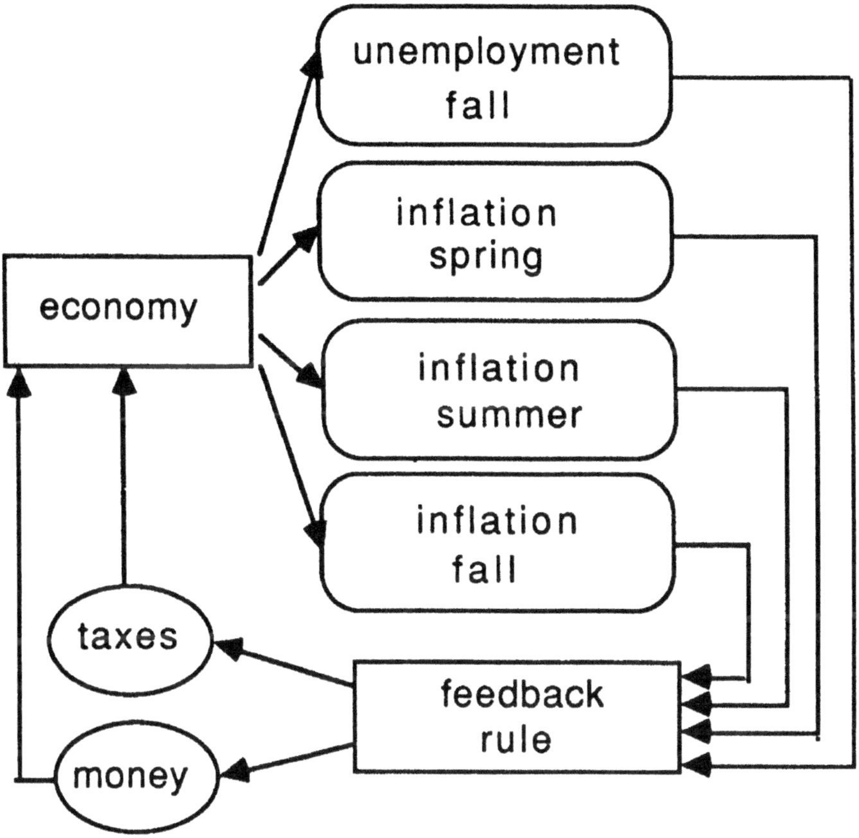

Figure 6.5. A Feedback Rule with Lags

Econometric models frequently have multiple lags. For example, the outlays for the construction of new plants are predicted most accurately by the interest rates in effect many quarters ago. This occurs because construction decisions are made on the basis of current interest rates but then it takes many quarters for the plans to be drawn, bids processed, and construction equipment assembled. Therefore, interest rates several quarters ago are the best predictors of current investment.

Policy determination in models with multiple lags yields feedback rules with lags that are as long as the lags in the models. Thus if the lag between money growth rates and inflation rates is three quarters, then the feedback rule will include inflation in three quarters prior to the current quarter.

This is an important point commonly ignored by those who use simple feedback rules that are not developed in the feedback framework. The simple rules always determine policy with last quarter's conditions and never recognize that efficient stabilization will require that conditions in several previous quarters determine the current policy.

In summary, simple feedback rules with one policy variable determined by one condition in the economy are not adequate. Rather the feedback framework produces feedback rules in which several policies are determined simultaneously by a variety of conditions in the economy. Moreover, the feedback rule will usually include not only current but also several recent past indicators of the condition of the economy.

7
Confidence Intervals Again

The results of the use of feedback rules can be shown with confidence intervals over time. Recall from Chapter 5 that the uncertainty about the response of consumers to tax changes could be described with confidence intervals that showed consumers' likely responses. Of course the con`sumer responses were uncertainty in the behavioral *input* to macroeconomic analysis. Here it is the *output* that is of interest — namely inflation and unemployment.

This chapter begins with a discussion of confidence intervals for unemployment rates. Then the second part of the chapter includes confidence intervals for both inflation and unemployment.

1. Feedback Rules and Dynamics

Before discussing the results of feedback analysis it is useful to examine the way in which the unemployment results are obtained. They are calculated by using the feedback rule from the previous chapter along with the dynamics of Chapter 4. The feedback rule is

unemployment (last quarter) ----> taxes (last quarter).

That is, the unemployment rate determines the level of

taxes. In contrast the dynamics are

taxes (last quarter) ----> unemployment (this quarter).

That is, taxes last quarter determine unemployment this quarter. When the feedback rule is used to replace taxes in the dynamics the resulting system is

unemployment (last quarter) ---> unemployment (this quarter).

That is, unemployment last quarter entirely determines unemployment this quarter because unemployment last quarter determines taxes through the feedback rule and then taxes determine unemployment this quarter.

However, *entirely* is too strong a word. *Substantially* would be more accurate. But what else has an effect on the evolution of unemployment over time? Uncertainty of course! Uncertainty in the form of shocks like crop failures and uncertainty in the form of behavioral responses. The result is that unemployment does not follow a single clearly determined path. The economist cannot say "Mr. President, if we use this feedback rule, the unemployment rate will decline gradually along this path for the next four quarters." All the economist can do is to present a chart like Figure 7.1 and say, "Mr. President, if we use this feedback rule there is an 80 percent probability that unemployment in each of the next four quarters will be in the ranges shown."

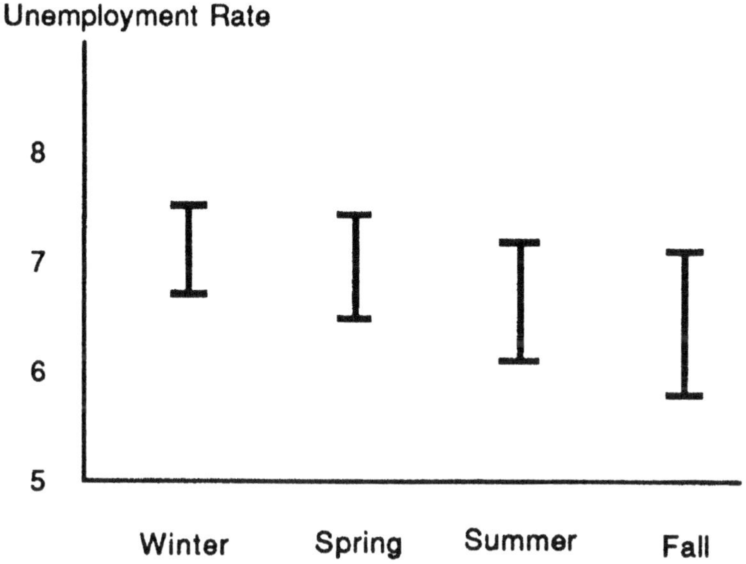

Figure 7.1. Confidence Intervals over Time

In fact, most presidents will not be content to see the results of using a single feedback rule; but rather, will want to know the likely outcome of using various types of feedback rules. Figure 7.2 is a chart of this kind.

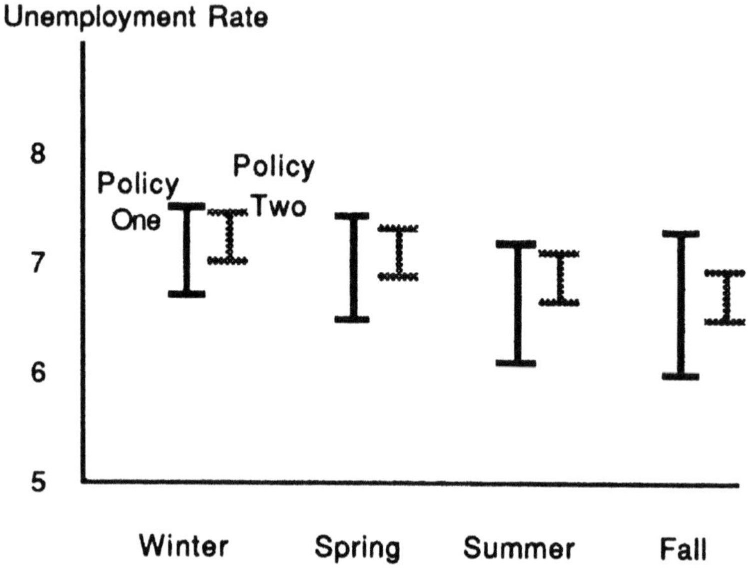

Figure 7.2. Confidence Intervals for Alternative Feedback Rules

Policy One is a more risky policy. It offers the possibility of unemployment rates as low as 6 percent by the fall before the election. It also carries the risk that the unemployment rate might be as high as 7.4 percent. In contrast Policy Two is less risky with the range of unemployment rates in the fall being 6.6 to 7.0 percent. Which policy will the President choose? It depends on the risk she is willing to take.

How do presidents now make this choice? Frequently, they are not given this choice. Instead, they are shown alternate paths and asked to choose between the paths. There is little discussion of alternate confidence intervals.

2. Inflation and Unemployment

The discussion between the President and her advisers does not focus on unemployment alone but also on inflation. How then does one display confidence intervals for inflation? Simply by replacing unemployment with inflation in Figure 7.1 above except that the confidence intervals would be wider since there is more uncertainty in inflation than in unemployment. However, it is useful to display both unemployment and inflation on the same graph as is done in Figure 7.3.

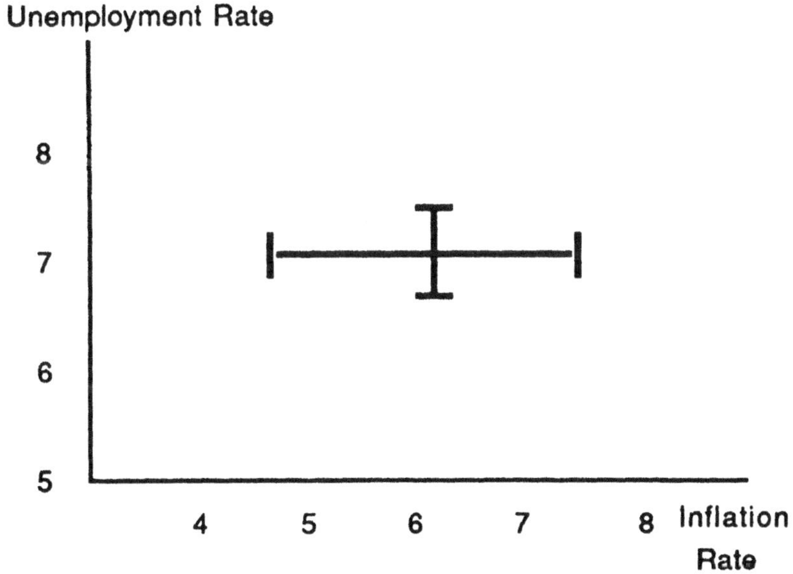

Figure 7.3. Confidence Intervals for Inflation and Unemployment

In Figure 7.3 unemployment is on one axis and inflation is

on the other. Thus the confidence interval for unemployment is the vertical line and the confidence interval for inflation is the horizontal line. Inflation has been displayed as being more uncertain than unemployment.

However, confidence intervals in two dimensions are not usually displayed with a cross but rather with an ellipse as is shown in Figure 7.4.

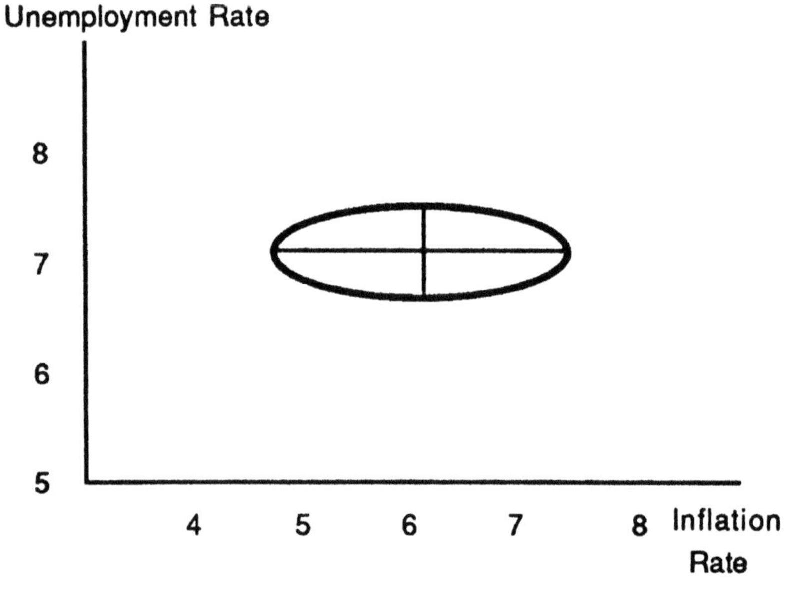

Figure 7.4. A Confidence Ellipse

The combinations of unemployment and inflation inside the ellipse are the 80 percent confidence interval.

In fact the ellipse would not usually have axes that are vertical and horizontal; rather the vertical axis would have a downward slope and the horizontal axis would have an upward slope. The axes are shown as vertical and horizontal here for the mutual convenience of the reader and the writer. They are easier for the reader to understand and easier for the writer to draw.

It is not usually a single ellipse that is of interest but rather a set of ellipses over time. Figure 7.5 shows ellipses for unemployment and inflation in the fall over a four-year Presidential term.

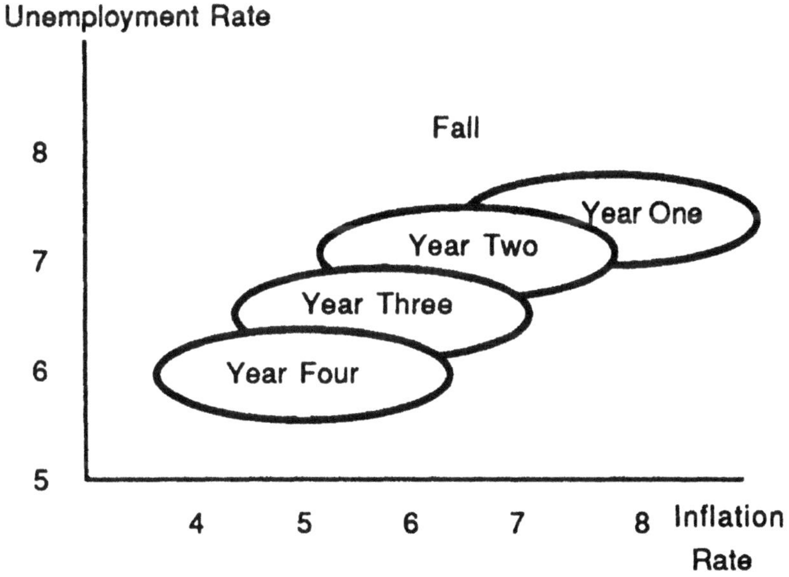

Figure 7.5. Confidence Ellipses over Time

In the fall of Year One the unemployment and inflation rates are both high but they gradually decrease over the four years of the Administration. In the fall of Year Four, just before the election, there is an 80 percent probability that unemployment would be between 5.2 and 6.3 percent and inflation between 3.7 and 7.3 percent *provided* a certain feedback rule is used.

Of course these ellipses will be much smaller if the feedback rules used depend more heavily on policies with little uncertainty. Thus a feedback rule that depended more heavily on taxes might have smaller ellipses than one that depended more heavily on monetary policy.

However, there is a minimum of uncertainty that no feedback rule can remove. This is the basic uncertainty from shocks and from behavior in response to even the most certain policy. This minimum of uncertainty may result in ellipses that are so large as to produce more modesty among economists than we sometimes exhibit. At the same time, the use of confidence ellipses may provide a much more accurate statement of the limits of economic understanding.

8
Automatic Stabilizers Revisited

The importance of the feedback framework is not so much in the full use of all the mathematical mechanics but rather in a frame of mind — a frame that considers dynamics, uncertainty, and feedback. Automatic stabilizers are a good example of the feedback style of thinking. This chapter provides a review of some existing stabilization policies and ideas for some new policies.

1. Unemployment Compensation

As was discussed earlier, the most well known automatic stabilizer is unemployment compensation. However, all unemployment compensation schemes are not equally efficient as automatic stabilizers. Some programs offer only a small compensation to workers and others offer a more generous compensation. In some programs the benefits are exhausted within a short period of time and in others the benefits last over longer periods of time. The Council of Economic Advisers during the Kennedy Administration realized the importance of automatic stabilizers and encouraged the President to strengthen them. This Council of Heller, Gordon, and Tobin pushed for an increase in both the amount of unemployment compensation and the period of eligibility. They even proposed a feedback rule under which there would be an extension of the benefit period when unemployment exceeded 5 percent and when more than 1 percent of the unemployed had exhausted their benefits. The campaign was successful and the stabilizing effects of the unemployment compensation system were strengthened during the Kennedy Administration.

2. Income Taxes

Another stabilizer the Council proposed concerned the income tax. They suggested and President Kennedy proposed to Congress a system under which the President could make small adjustments in income tax rates in response to changes in the unemployment rate. If Congress had approved it, this legislation would have decreased the length of the decision lag for tax policy by four to six months. However, Congress rejected the idea because it saw this proposal as giving away its Constitutional right to levy taxes.

This idea surfaced again during Reagan's first term in office in a form that was much more acceptable to Congress — indeed it was even suggested by Congressman Dan Rostenkowski, chairman of the Ways and Means Committee. Congress had adopted Reagan's proposal for a 25 percent cut in the personal income tax but had phased it over a two-and-a-half-year period in steps of 5, 10, and 10 percent. After the 5 and the 10 percent cuts had gone into effect Congressman Rostenkowski proposed that the last 10 percent should go in effect only if certain conditions were met to trigger the action. These conditions were

- a fiscal year 1983 unified budget deficit of $22.9 billion or less.
- a consumer price index for the third quarter of 1983 of 309 or less.
- a 90-day Treasury bill rate for the third quarter of 1983 of 7.5% or less.

Unless all three of these tests were met the last phase of the tax cut would not go into effect. This was a feedback idea. The action would have occurred only if a certain condition was met and would have occurred without further Congressional debate.

Tax legislation sets tax rates. However, this legislation would have been different. It would have set tax rates that depended on conditions in the economy. If Congressman Rostenkowski's proposal had been adopted, we would have had the beginning of a feedback rule for income tax rates.

Yet another feedback idea was put forward by Heller, Gordon, and Tobin. This idea was about public works and it too was not approved at the time.

3. Public Works

Under the present system of public-works legislation the President proposes and Congress votes funds for particular projects. The sum of the cost of the projects approved is then the total expenditure on public works. This sum has little or nothing to do with the level of unemployment.

Feedback

This system could be converted to a feedback system if the amount of public-works expenditure varied from year to year depending on the levels of unemployment and inflation as is illustrated in Figure 8.1.

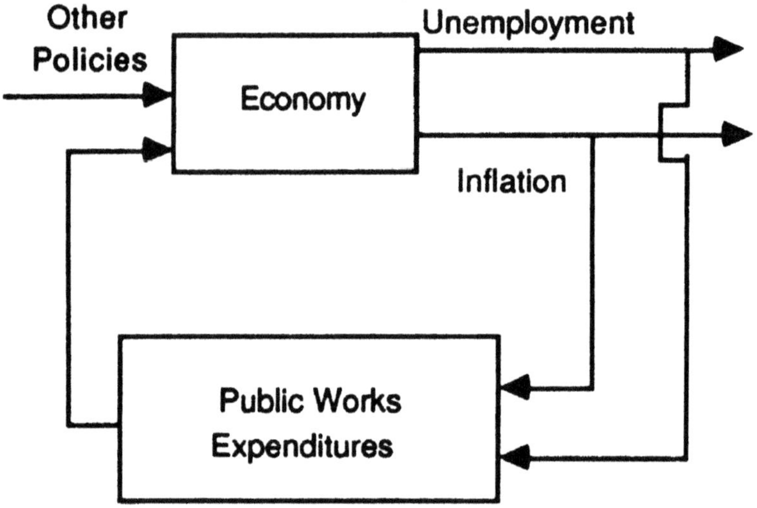

Figure 8.1. Feedback in Public-Works Expenditure

Congress and the President could still determine the position of public-works projects within a priority list, but the number of projects funded each year would be a feedback function of such conditions in the economy as the unemployment and inflation rates.

4. Agricultural Programs

Another area where feedback rules could be helpful is agricultural policy. Support prices are now fixed without regard for macroeconomics and yet agricultural prices play a particularly important role in determining the rate of inflation.

The feedback rules for agricultural support prices would be determined not so much by unemployment as by inflation and by the supply-and-demand situation for food and fibers. Also, sales from or purchases to buffer stocks would play an important role in agricultural stabilization with feedback rules.

5. Labor-Market Policy

When unemployment reaches high levels, public employment programs are sometimes created. The most famous of these programs were used by Roosevelt during the Great Depression. More recent examples are the job training and employment programs that existed as recently as the Carter Administration.

The programs in the Carter Administration provided a good example of a time when the feedback approach would have been useful. When President Carter entered office the unemployment rate was 7 percent. His Secretary of Labor, Ray Marshall, suggested large public employment programs. These programs were eventually proposed by the President and then debated at length and passed by Congress. Finally, the machinery was set up in the Labor Department to administer the programs. The result of this long lag was that the programs gained full operational and funding strength just when they were not needed. By the time they were fully in effect, inflation and not unemployment was the key problem in the economy. Then another two years later the Reagan Administration entered office and eliminated the programs, just as unemployment approached 10 percent. In contrast to what actually happened, if the original legislation had been drafted to tie the level of expenditure on the program to the level of unemployment, then the program would have contracted or expanded as needed in a timely way.

This legislation is an example of the contrast between feedback control methods and the policy procedures we now use. When an airplane first begins to veer off course the automatic pilot immediately begins to apply small corrective action — slowly and smoothly. When the economy goes off course the President delays in proposing action until he is sure that that the problem is serious. Then Congress debates the appropriate action for months. Finally the problem has become so serious that strong measures are approved and the economy is jerked back sharply toward the desired course. However, because of the lags there is too much medicine too late and the economy overshoots its desired course and eventually must be jerked back in the opposite direction.

6. Decreasing the Decision Lag

The country suffers longer periods of high unemployment than would be necessary if the long decision lags in taxation and expenditure policy could be decreased. Unemployment compensation is an example of a current policy with no decision lag. Several examples are given above of various means to decrease decision lags in a variety of policy areas without either the Congress or the Administration giving up their power to oversee the operation of the economy.

As an additional incentive for policymakers to decrease the decision lag we need to create some new indices. One such measure would be the number of person-months of unemployment. A 10 percent unemployment rate with a labor force of 100 million means ten million people unemployed. If such a rate persisted for three months the result would be thirty million person-months of unemployment. Using such an index one could measure the decrease in misery that could be won with shorter decision lags. For example, policies that shortened the debate in the Administration and Congress by six months and reduced the unemployment rate by even one percent would reduce the unemployment misery index by six million person-months. While you sit in the quiet comfort of your office or study you may pass over this statistic with ease. But stop a minute. Try to think how miserable you would be if you wanted work and were not able to find it for six months. Think of your loss of self-esteem and your concern about the welfare of your family. Then multiply that misery by one million.

7. Checking with the Full Framework

Finally, one caution about automatic stabilizers. Feedback rules can be destabilizing as well as stabilizing. For example, a feedback rule that raised taxes in response to rises in unemployment would be destabilizing. Also, the lags in the economy and in the operation of the feedback rule can result in destabilizing behavior. Therefore it is important that the mathematical mechanics of the feedback framework be used in order to assure that various automatic stabilizers proposed are indeed stabilizing and that there is proper coordination between policies. Consequently the full feedback framework need not be used to develop ideas for stabilizers but much of this framework should be used to be certain that the rules developed will have their desired effects.

In summary, the feedback framework offers the possibility of substantial improvements in the operation of macroeconomic policy. However, feedback methods are not without their limitations. These limitations are discussed in the next four chapters.

Part III
Limitations

All too frequently in economics a new approach is advocated without an accompanying statement of the limitations of the approach. The limitations eventually emerge in the course of the public debate but the process is protracted. Here some of the limitations of the feedback approach are discussed in order to permit you to weigh carefully the pros and cons. These limitations are

- choice of criterion
- reactions to policy
- choice of model
- multiple decision makers.

The desired paths and weights discussed in Chapter 3 constitute a particular goal or choice of criterion. Many economists would prefer to use various other criteria for selecting among policies.

How people will react to policy is an old topic in economics — as old as public policy discussions. An example from the last fifty years is the debate that arose from Keynes' consumption function. Part of that debate concerned what proportion of increases in income that consumers would spend. More recently proponents of rational expectations have argued that feedback rules will be invalid as soon as they are announced because consumers and producers will change their behavior as soon as they know the feedback rule.

The choice of model is a difficult problem in economics since controlled experiments cannot be run. Many false models can be rejected with statistical procedures; however, sometimes two or more models fit the data equally well, so it is difficult or impossible to ascertain which competitor is indeed the correct model. Since the feedback rules reflect the choice of model, it is equally difficult to determine which is the correct feedback rule among those obtained from competing models.

Finally, one person does not control economic policy but rather the control extends to many people in the Administration, in Congress, and on the Federal Reserve Board. The simple approach to feedback that uses only a single decision maker is therefore incomplete.

Some of these limitations of the feedback approach can be mitigated within its framework with ease. Others can be mitigated only with considerable effort. Still others are limitations that are impossible to ease or to remove. The following chapters provide a guided tour of these four kinds of limitations.

9
The Choice of Criterion

One of the limitations of the feedback framework is that there are many ways to specify the criterion for choosing the best policy or policies. Thus there are a variety of opinions among the experts about how best to specify the criterion function. This chapter will chart the terrain of opinions about the best form for the criterion function, the choice of weights, and the choice of desired paths.

1. The Form of the Criterion Function

The most common form of the criterion function is called the quadratic. This means that the function includes squared terms. For example, it includes a term like

$$(\text{actual unemployment - desired unemployment})^2$$

— that is, the square of the difference between actual and desired unemployment. The criterion is minimized so the objective is to make the squared term above as small as possible by having the actual and desired levels of unemployment be as close to one another as possible .

In the quadratic function above, if the actual unemployment level was 8 percent and the desired unemployment rate was 4 percent, this part of the function would be

$$(8 - 4)^2 = (4)^2 = 16.$$

Or if the actual unemployment level were 10 percent, it would be

$$(10 - 4)^2 = (6)^2 = 36.$$

A plot of these penalties is given in Figure 9.1.

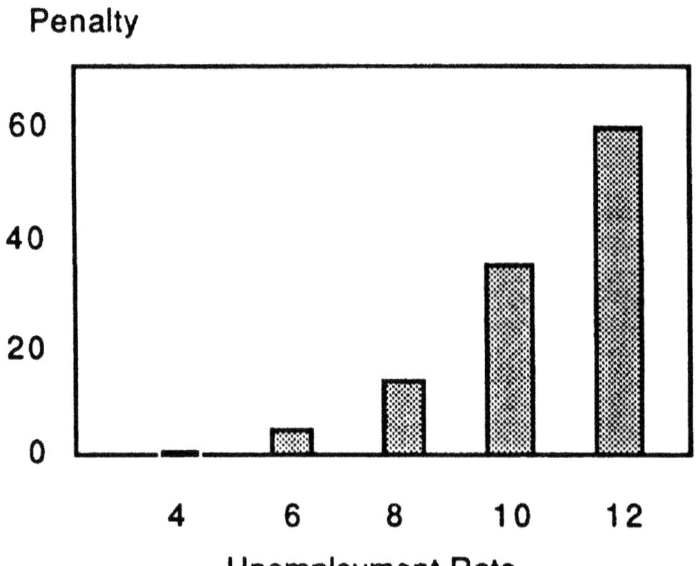

Fig. 9.1. A Quadratic Criterion Function for Unemployment

The value of the function is called a *penalty* because it is a measure of the deviation of the actual path from the desired path. The greater the deviation, the greater the penalty. Consequently the penalty is zero when the actual unemployment and the desired unemployment rate are both 4 percent. Also, as computed above, the penalty is 16 when the actual unemployment rate is 8 and the penalty is 36 when the actual unemployment rate is 10.

This form of the criterion function seems reasonable enough until Figure 9.1 is extended a little to the left so that you can look at the penalty in the range from 0 to 4 percent unemployment. This is shown in Figure 9.2.

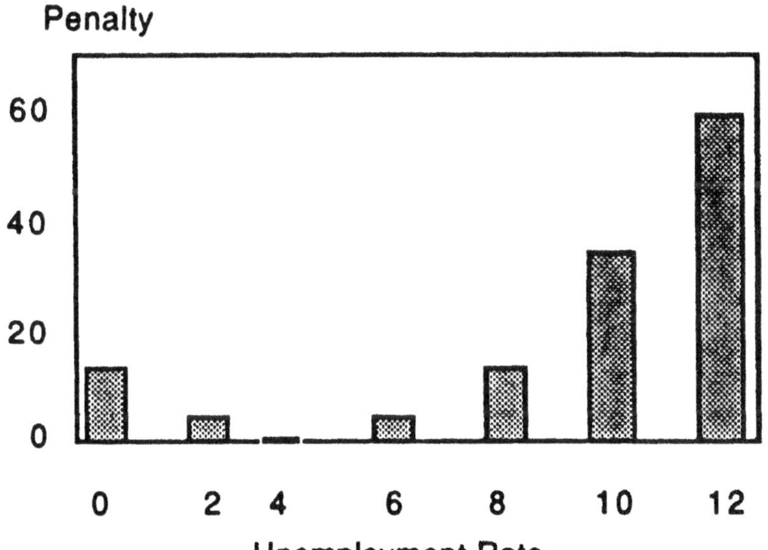

Figure 9.2. Two Sides of the Quadratic Penalty Function

There is a penalty for exceeding the desired unemployment rate of 4 percent, but there is also a penalty for having a rate *below* 4 percent. This is clearly undesirable.

A simple way to ease this limitation is to shift the desired level of unemployment to the left. The resulting function is displayed in Figure 9.3 where the desired level of unemployment is changed from 4 percent to 2 percent.

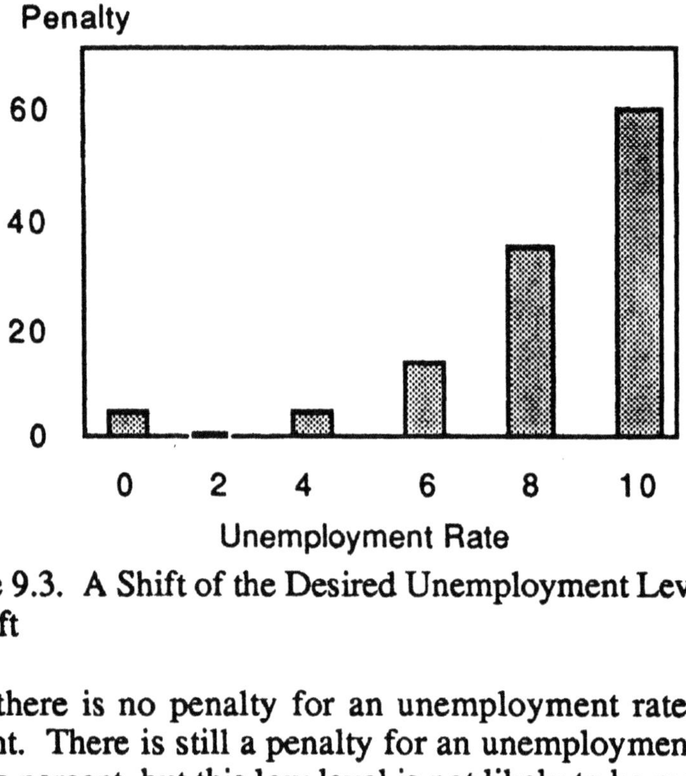

Figure 9.3. A Shift of the Desired Unemployment Level to the Left

Now there is no penalty for an unemployment rate of 2 percent. There is still a penalty for an unemployment rate of zero percent, but this low level is not likely to be reached so it presents no problem.

A more difficult way to ease the limitation is to have the function be asymmetric about the desired level of unemployment, that is the function will have different shapes on the two sides of the desired level of unemployment. This requires the use of two quadratic functions — one to the right of the desired level and one to the left. The function to the left would be flat and near zero while the one to the right would be rising steeply.

So the quadratic function can be modified to meet some of the objections that are raised to its use. However, there is another problem. Quadratic functions always look like bowls — they rise more and more steeply from the center to the rim of the bowl as is shown in Figure 9.4.

Figure 9.4. A Quadratic Penalty Function for Unemployment

This figure is plotted with a line instead of with a bar graph in order to emphasize the curvature of the function. Also, the desired level has been shifted back to 4 percent again to be consistent with Figure 9.2.

The objection to this form of the criterion is a lack of flexibility. For example, some argue that the criterion function should not rise ever more steeply but should level off at some point as shown in Figure 9.5.

Figure 9.5. A More General Criterion Function

Greater flexibility is to be preferred provided it costs nothing. However, with present methods the cost of moving away from the quadratic function to other forms is high: it requires in most cases that uncertainty be eliminated from the analysis. Thus the confidence intervals and ellipses that were discussed earlier cannot be used. Rather the discussion of the policy must be deterministic — without uncertainty.

The result of this choice is that most models without

uncertainty use general nonlinear criterion functions and most models with uncertainty use quadratic criterion functions. Therefore one limitation that arises from the choice of criterion functions is the form of the function — quadratic or general nonlinear.

When the quadratic function is used another limitation arises, namely the choice of weights.

2. Choice of Weights

The greatest difficulty with the choice of weights is the process of choosing them. This problem was discussed at length in Chapter 3, so it is only necessary to summarize the problem and the solution here. The problem is that policymakers may have a difficult time assigning relative weights to inflation and unemployment. However, the same problem arises in the use of weights in the design of engineering feedback control systems. In engineering the solution to the problem is to do computer simulations with various weights until a satisfactory design is obtained. The same thing can be done in economic systems by using computer simulations with different weights until the policymakers are pleased with the outcome. Also, even after the weights are chosen opinions about them will change with time and with economic events so that it will be necessary to change them with the passage of time.

There is a final limitation that springs from the choice of quadratic criterion function. This is the choice of desired paths.

3. Choice of Desired Paths

Some economists feel that it is difficult for policymakers to choose desired paths for unemployment, inflation, and the government deficit and that this is therefore one of the limitations of the feedback framework. Others disagree.

They think most policymakers find it relatively easy to articulate the paths they want the economy to follow. Moreover, they think an open discussion about desired paths has a salutary effect on the democratic process. It permits a clear statement of goals at the beginning of the Presidential term and a means to measure performance at the end of the term.

So, for many economists, this limitation is not a limitation but rather a strength of the feedback approach. However, for those who think that policymakers will be unable or unwilling to describe desired paths this remains a significant limitation.

10
Reactions to Policy

Reactions to policy have been of interest to economists for many years. However, concern about these reactions has taken a new form recently and has received considerable attention from the school of rational-expectations economists. One of the concerns of this school has been that feedback rules cannot be used for policy because the announcement of the rule will cause people to change their behavior which means that a different rule should have been proposed. These concerns are viewed by many as an important limitation of the feedback framework. Therefore they will be discussed in this chapter beginning with an earlier interest in reactions to policy and proceeding to the recent discussion.

As an illustration of these earlier lines of research consider the simple form of the consumption function where

consumption = (percentage consumed) (disposable income)

Consumption is determined by multiplying the percentage consumed times disposable income. Thus, if a consumer has a disposable (after-tax) income of $3,000 per month and saves 10 percent and consumes 90 percent of this amount, his consumption will be

$$\$2700 = (.90)\ (\$3000)$$

that is, $2,700 per month.

Now what will be the consumer's reaction to changes in policy? Two kinds of reactions may be distinguished — one when the percentage consumed changes and the other when disposable income changes. On the surface the difference in these two reactions may seem rather small. However, the difference is sharp in economic models as is shown in the equation below

	parameter	variable
consumption =	(percentage consumed)	(disposable income)

The percentage consumed is a behavioral parameter and is assumed to remain constant over time. In contrast, disposable income is a variable and is assumed to vary over time. Although economic models are built on the assumption that variables will change and parameters will remain constant, changes of both variables *and* parameters are discussed here.

1. Changes in Variables

When the government cuts taxes, disposable income increases and the consumer reacts by increasing his consumption. As disposable income changes, consumption changes in response but the percentage consumed remains constant:

consumption = (percentage consumed)***(disposable income)***

This is the most common form of reaction to policy in macroeconomic models. Other examples of this kind of reaction are (1) the money supply is changed and interest rates react and (2) exchange rates are changed and imports and exports react. In all of these cases policy variables are changed and other variables change in response but parameters do not change. Next consider the recent discussion about parameter changes.

2. Changes in Parameters

When the government announces a feedback rule, consumers may react by changing their percentage consumed. This in turn will cause a change in consumption even if disposable income remains constant:

consumption = ***(percentage consumed)*** (disposable income)

What could cause consumers to change their percentage consumed? Suppose the government announced a feedback rule that indicated taxes would be increased in response to increases in inflation. Then if consumers expected an increase in inflation, they would also expect an increase in taxes. Therefore they might decrease their percentage consumed and save more in order to have a larger buffer if taxes were to be increased. Thus the announcement of the feedback rule could cause a change in behavior, that is, a change in a parameter of the economic model.

Now why is this a limitation on the use of the feedback

framework? The beginning of the answer is shown in Figure 10.1.

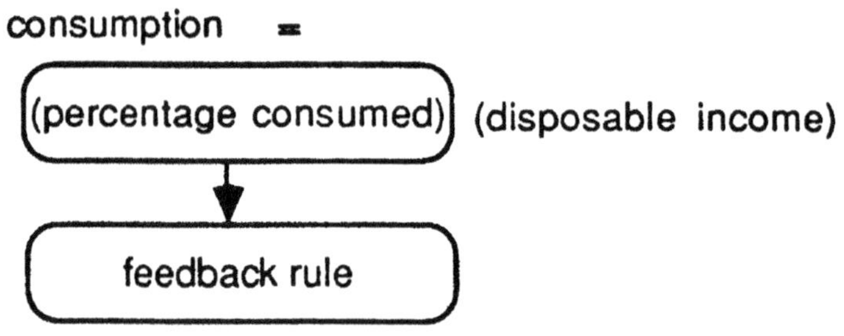

Figure 10.1. Determination of the Feedback Rule

This figure shows that the feedback rule is determined by the percentage consumed parameter. This seems reasonable because the feedback rules should reflect the behavior of consumers and producers.

But if the use of the feedback rule alters behavioral, it not only is *determined by* but also *determines* behavioral parameters. This is illustrated in Figure 10.2. The percentage consumed at the top of the figure determines the feedback rule. Then the government announces the feedback rule and consumers change their behavior in response to the announcement. This change in behavior is shown in the bottom half of the figure. Furthermore, the change in behavior determines a new and different feedback rule.

Consequently one of the concerns of the proponents of rational expectations has been that feedback rules induce behavioral changes that in turn imply additional changes in the feedback rule. They point to this as a major difference between the use of feedback rules with airplanes and with consumers. When a feedback rule for an airplane is announced, the airplane does not change its behavior.

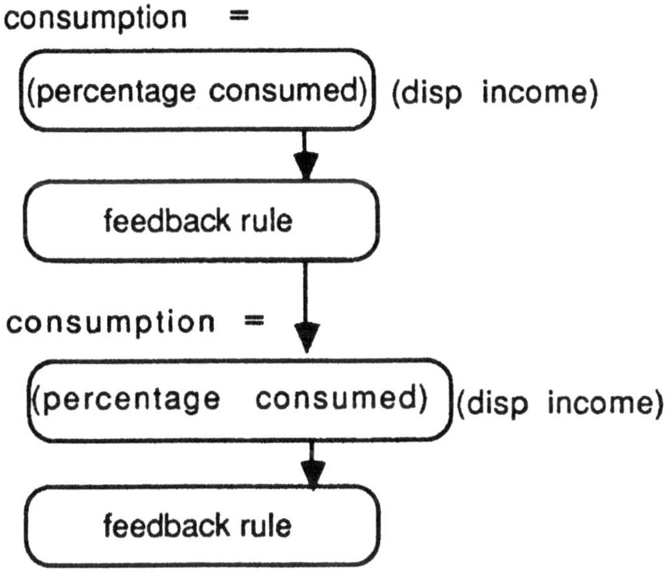

Figure 10.2. Reaction to the Announcement of the Feedback Rule

However, when a feedback rule affecting consumers is announced, the consumers may change their spending and saving patterns.

Then what, if anything, can be done to modify the simple feedback framework to ease this limitation? There are two possible approaches. One approach is easy but incomplete and the other is complete but difficult.

The easy approach is for the government to track the

changing behavior of consumers in response to the feedback rule and to continue to modify the rule so long as consumer behavior continues to change. For example, if the government announces a feedback rule that causes consumers to change their behavior, then the government must compute a new feedback rule based on the altered behavior. The announcement of the new rule may cause additional changes in behavior and therefore require the computation of yet another feedback rule. Therefore this approach is easy to implement but incomplete because the feedback rule is always one step behind the change in behavior. However, if the change in behavior at each step is not large the feedback rule in use at each point in time will not differ much from the optimal feedback rule.

The second approach is more difficult. In determining the feedback rule the government anticipates that consumers will change their behavior in response to the announcement of the rule. So even the first feedback rule used by the government anticipates that consumers will react to the announcement of the policy and accordingly allows for that reaction. One problem with this approach is that consumers may expect that the government will do this and modify their behavior in anticipation. What arises is a game between the government and consumers as shown in Figure 10.3 as they eye each other's behavior.

In choosing their behavior both government and consumers anticipate that the other will anticipate that the other will anticipate that . . . Games of this form can be analyzed by economists, but the analysis is complicated.

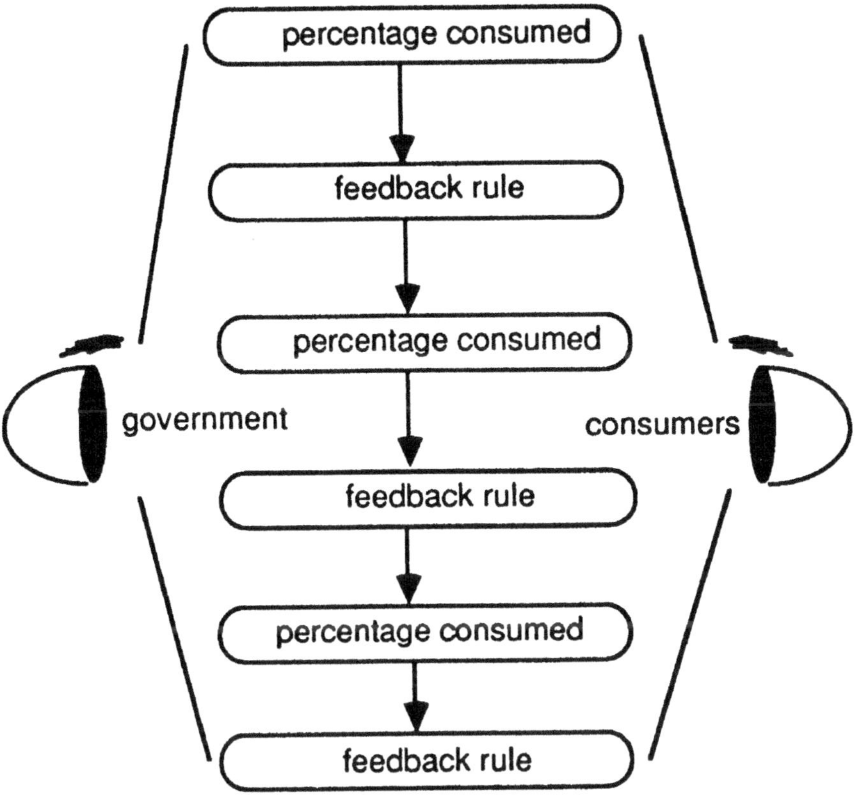

Figure 10.3. The Government and Consumers Eye Each Other's Behavior

Considerable research is now being conducted on this problem and it is possible that simple forms of game analysis can be developed.

Neither of these two approaches to easing the limitation caused by behavioral change may be necessary. If the reaction of consumers to the announcement of the feedback rule is *small*, then that reaction can be ignored in determining the feedback rule. Economists do not yet know the size of behavioral reactions to the announcement of feedback rules. Empirical research is in progress and will doubtless continue for some time. Meanwhile there is considerable hope that the size of the reactions are small enough that the simple forms of feedback analysis can be used without either of these compensating approaches.

11
The Choice of Model

Economists cannot run controlled experiments. The economy is not like a garden that can be divided into sections and different amounts of fertilizer applied to each section in order to determine the effects of the fertilizer. Economists cannot change one factor at a time in order to study its effect on the economy. Rather we must make do with the data that are generated as the economy evolves.

Since we cannot run controlled experiments, we have difficulty in determining the true model of the economy. Rival groups each can claim that their model is the correct model of the economy, but both models cannot be correct. Sometimes the data is sufficient to permit tests to determine that one or both models are not correct. In other cases, however, the two models may fit the data equally well and so we cannot be sure which is the more accurate model. Controlled experiments cannot be used to determine which is the true model. Therefore we must live with some ambiguity about which is the correct model of the economy.

Models from which we choose may differ in two ways: (1) they may include different variables and (2) they may have the same variables but different forms of functions.

Feedback

1. Different Variables

One model may include a consumption function in which disposable income alone determines consumption:

Another model may have a more complicated consumption function in which both disposable income, that is, after-tax income, and wealth, viz stocks and bonds, determine consumption:

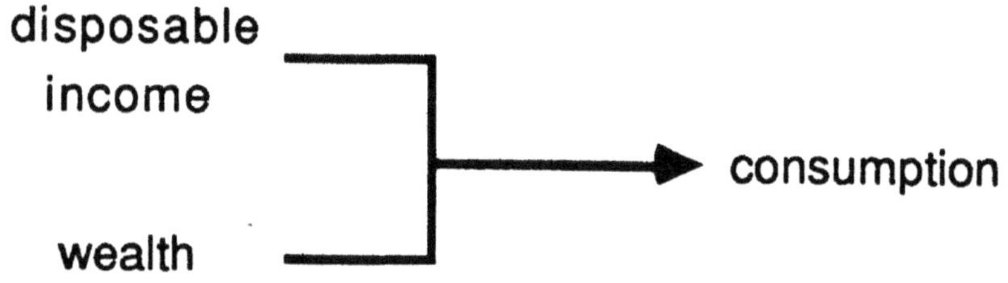

The data may not be sufficient to permit economists to determine which of these two is the true model.

But perhaps it does not matter which is the true model. Oh, but it does! As Figure 11.1 shows one way fiscal policy works is by changing taxes to affect disposable income and therefore consumption.

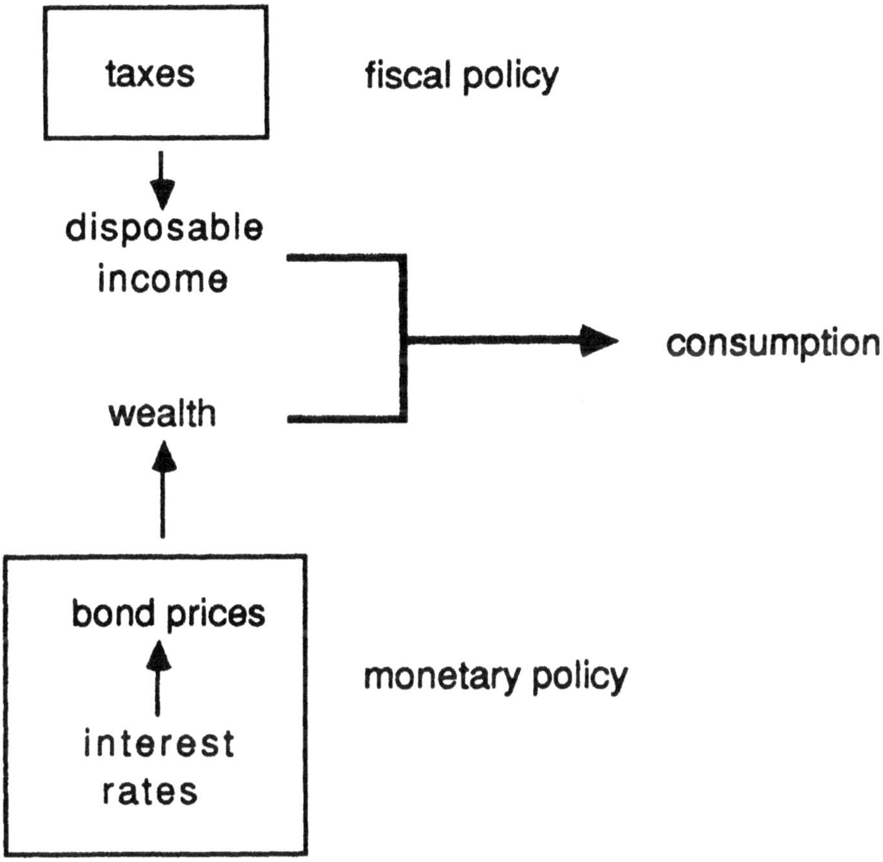

Figure 11.1. Fiscal and Monetary Policy

In contrast, monetary policy works by altering interest rates and bond prices to change wealth. The change in wealth then affects consumption. So in the simple model monetary policy has no effect on consumption. But in the more complicated model monetary policy does have an effect on consumption. Consequently the presence or absence of wealth from the consumption function makes a big difference in the choice of policy. But the data may not be sufficient to determine which is the best model and which therefore is the best policy.

In most cases the data are sufficient to determine whether or not a variable should be included in an equation. For example, someone might propose that exchange rates should be included in the consumption function. Statistical tests could be performed with the data that would indicate whether or not exchange rates have a significant effect on consumption.

So the data are sufficient to rule out many variables. Even though we can eliminate many variables, at times we are still left with a few crucial variables for which the data are not adequate for us to decide whether to include them in the equation.

2. Form

A second problem of model choice arises when we can determine which variables are in the equations but we cannot be sure of the form or shape of some of the functions. An example is shown in Figure 11.2.

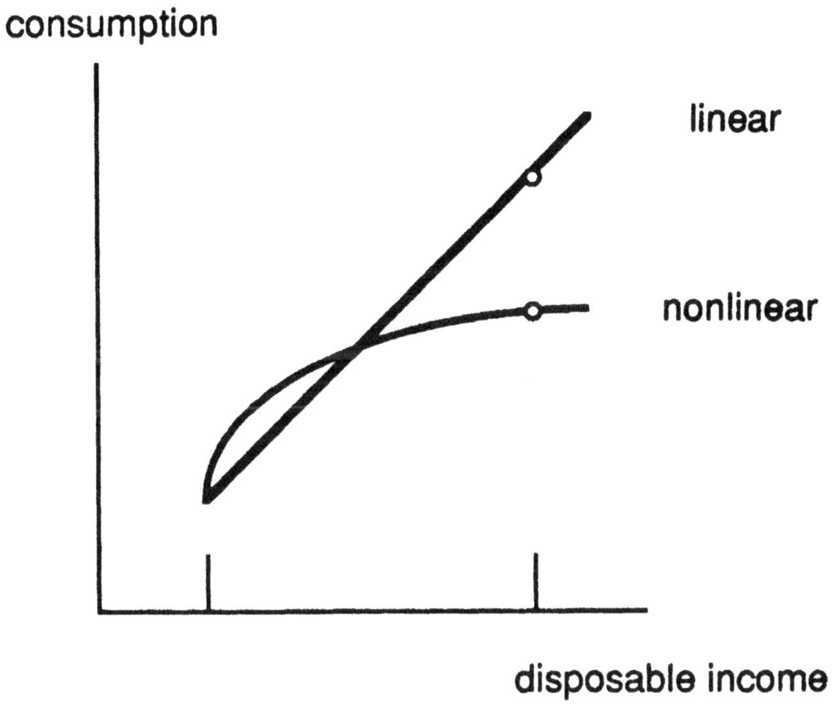

Figure 11.2. Linear and Nonlinear Consumption Functions

The straight line shows consumption as a linear function of disposable income. In contrast the curved line shows consumption as a nonlinear function of income. At some levels of disposable income it may not matter which is the true form of the function — for example, it does not matter which function is used at the points that the two functions cross. However, at the point where the two small circles are shown it does matter. Here the nonlinear function suggests that a much lower level of consumption will occur than would be predicted with the linear function. Thus a much larger tax cut would be required with the nonlinear function to have the same stimulating effect on the economy as with the linear function.

In most cases it is possible to show that one form is better than another. However, some ambiguity about the correct shape of the function remains at times, even after all the appropriate statistical tests are employed.

So what is to be done when we cannot determine which among several models is the correct model? One approach is to make use of multiple models.

3. Use of Multiple Models

The Federal Reserve Board (FRB) maintains a large econometric model of the economy. Also, some private firms like Data Resources Inc. (DRI) have developed models of the economy and the Council of Economic Advisers may use portions of its own model as well as draw from those developed by others. Consequently several models of the economy may be in use at one time. The models are different and so are the feedback rules that can be calculated from the models. Then how should one use these various models?

One approach is to pool the information contained in the models. Another approach is to use the feedback rule from only one model and to select the rule that causes the least harm. Harm arises if you use the feedback rule from one model when another model is actually the correct model of the economy. Of course we do not know and cannot know for sure what is the correct model of the economy. However, we can analyze the consequences if it should happen to be true that one of the models was indeed the correct model.

Thus one can construct a figure showing the results of using the feedback rule from a model if the true state of the economy were as envisaged by each of the models. This is done for the FRB feedback rule in Figure 11.3. Consider first the 100 in the left-hand box. This is the penalty cost when the FRB model is used to derive the feedback rule and the true state of the economy is as envisaged by that model.

		True State of the Economy		
		Federal Reserve Board	Council of Economic Advisers	Data Resources Inc.
Model Used	Federal Reserve Board	100	125	110

Figure 11.3. Cost of Using the FRB Feedback Rule When the True State of the Economy is as Envisaged by Each Model

"Penalty cost" is the criterion value which was discussed in Chapter 9. It is a measure of the separation between the actual and the desired paths. The greater the separation between the actual and the desired paths the greater the penalty cost. The second block in Figure 11.3 shows that the penalty cost would be 125 if the feedback rule from the FRB model were used when the true state of the economy was that expected by the Council of Economic Advisers (CEA) model. Consequently, if the FRB feedback rule were used and the true state of the economy was as expected by the CEA the separation between the actual and the desired paths would be greater and therefore the penalty cost would be greater. Finally, if the FRB feedback rule were used and the economy were as expected by the Data Resources, Inc. model, the penalty cost would be 110.

Figure 11.3 can then be extended to include rows which show the consequences of using the other two feedback rules. This is done in Figure 11.4. The numbers shown in these figures are not the actual outcome of an experiment using these three models, rather they are illustrative of the way in which such experiments are performed.

Model Used \ True State of the Economy	Federal Reserve Board	Council of Economic Advisers	Data Resources Inc.
Federal Reserve Board	100	125 *	110
Council of Economic Advisers	120	80	140 *
Data Resources Inc.	135	160 *	120

Figure 11.4. Minimizing the Harm

The rows show the model used and the columns show the model that might be the true state of thc economy. The second row then shows the penalty cost which would occur if the CEA model were used and each of the three models represented the true state of the economy. The last row shows the same thing for the use of the DRI feedback rule.

Since there is uncertainty about the true state of the economy, which is the best feedback rule to use? One answer to this question is to use the feedback rule that would do the least harm. Examining the starred squares in Figure 11.4 reveals that the worst outcome using the FRB rule is 125. The worst outcome for the CEA rule would be 140 and the worst outcome for the DRI rule would be 160. Therefore the strategy that causes the least harm is to use the FRB feedback rule. Then no matter what is the true model, the performance of the economy would be no worse than 125. Thus the most robust feedback rule would be used — most robust in the sense that it would make the economy perform reasonably well, no matter what the true state of the economy is.

Consider a simple example from the consumption functions discussed in the first section of this chapter. The feedback rule from the model with only disposable income in the consumption function might be used instead of the feedback rule from the model with both disposable income and wealth in the consumption function. The first feedback rule might be the most robust since it would not rely on the functioning of monetary policy that might or might not work.

This area of model choice is one in which there is still considerable discussion among scholars about the best approach to use. For example, the objection is raised against the approach outlined above that the three models used did not encompass the principal types of model specifications so more models would need to be added. Another objection is that the addition of a poor and irrelevant model might cause the best model to be rejected and an inferior model to be used.

4. Changing Structure of the Economy

Even if we were able to determine the true model, it might soon be outdated by the changing structure of the economy. So it is not sufficient to determine the correct model once — rather it is necessary to continue to determine the correct model as the economy changes.

Following the OPEC embargo in 1973 there was a change in the economy of the following sort. Before the change, the structure of inflation was

capacity shortages ⟶ inflation

If an effort was made to produce too many goods in an overheated economy, capacity shortages would cause inflation. So the feedback rule indicated that the way to slow inflation was to increase taxes or decrease government expenditures. This would decrease the capacity shortages and slow the inflation. In contrast, after the change the

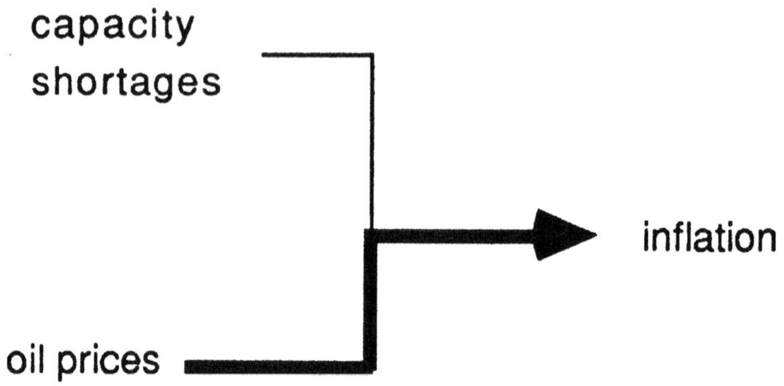

inflation was caused primarily by increases in world oil prices.

At that time even large models of the economy did not explicitly include oil prices. However, an independent observer might have correctly perceived the change in the structure of the economy and attributed the inflation to the increase in oil prices. The independent observer might have realized that increasing taxes or cutting government expenditures would not decrease prices since the inflation was almost entirely due to the rise in oil prices and not to capacity shortages.

This situation was a useful warning to all of us who use models. We must develop modeling systems that are friendly enough that the models can be manipulated with facility. The models must be such that economists can comprehend them with ease. The computer software must be friendly enough that the models can be modified quickly.

In summary, there are times when it is not possible to determine which is the correct model. When this occurs economists may use averages of the models or may decide to use that model that causes the least harm. Determining the correct model is not the economists' only problem; we must also modify our models if the economy changes.

12
Multiple Decision Makers

The simple feedback framework includes a single decision maker like the pilot of an airplane or a spacecraft. However, the economy is influenced by the decisions of many. Not only the President and Congress but also the FRB determine policy for the economy. Moreover, it's not only decisions in the public sector but also decisions in the private sector that determine the level of economic activity.

Economists have studied the problem of generalizing the feedback framework to include multiple decision makers. These studies have focused first on the President and Congress, who make fiscal policy, and the Federal Reserve Board, which determines monetary policy. However, the President and Congress constitute a group of decision makers and the conflicts within this group have been less well analyzed. Finally, the conflicts between public and private decision makers have received considerable attention of late under the name of rational expectations. This last topic has already been discussed in Chapter 10.

1. The President and Congress versus the FRB

The Federal Reserve Board is responsible for monetary policy while the President and Congress together determine fiscal policy. An important difference between monetary and fiscal policy is illustrated in Figure 12.1

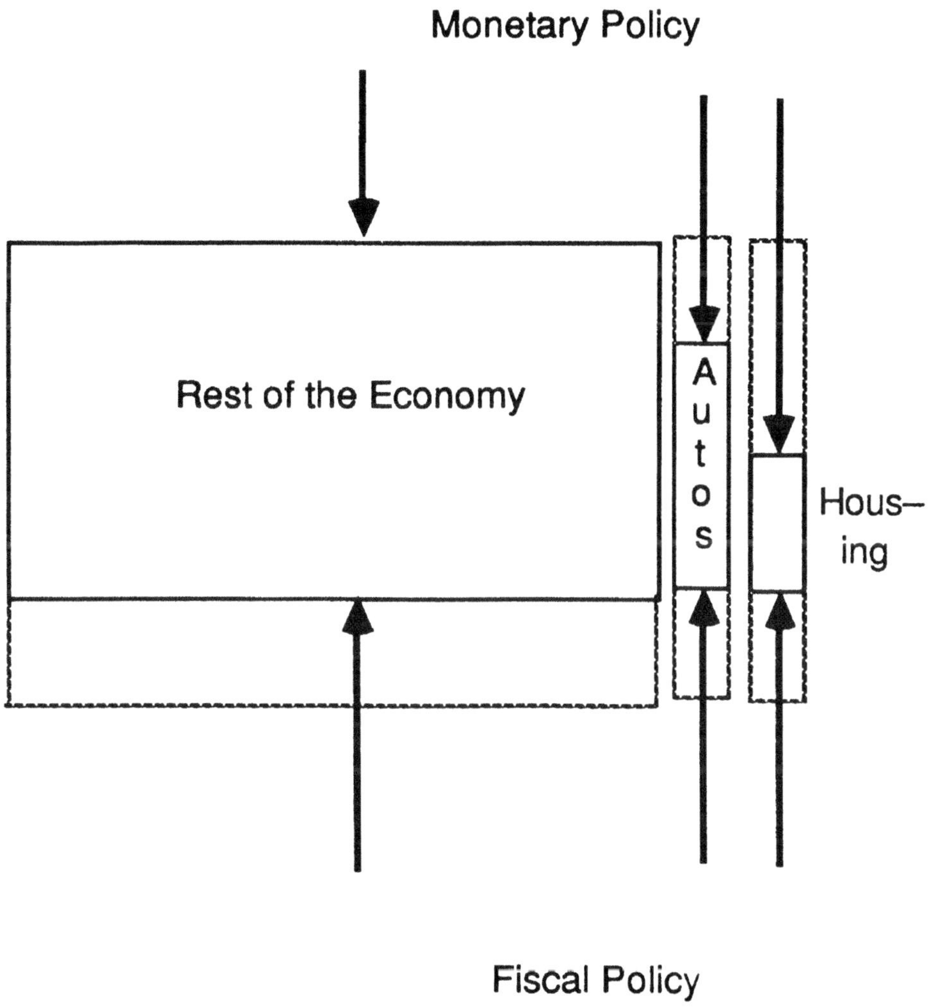

Figure 12.1. Effects of Monetary and Fiscal Policy

Feedback

One of the principal ways monetary policy affects the economy is through interest rates. When the FRB slows the growth of the money supply, interest rates rise. This causes sharp contractions in the housing and automobile industry but may have little or no effect on the rest of the economy. Consequently, an effort by the FRB to slow inflation can result in sharp contractions in the housing and automobile industry and little change in the rest of the economy. In contrast, fiscal policy which used taxes and government spending has a broad impact across the whole economy. If taxes are increased almost every sector of the economy will contract. So a conflict between the FRB on the one hand and the President and Congress on the other hand is an unequal match. The FRB can slow the economy but only by causing drastic reductions in the housing and automobile industries.

Conflict between the FRB and the President and Congress sometimes occurs because the FRB is more concerned about inflation and less concerned about unemployment than are the President and Congress. The situation is made more difficult by the fact that the President and Congress are using one group of econometric models and the Federal Reserve Board is using another model. The FRB model of course focuses more heavily on the role of monetary policy and may even portray monetary policy as more effective than do the models used by the President and Congress.

Timing is one other dimension in which the FRB differs from the President and Congress. The FRB can and does review and change policy almost monthly while the President and Congress make economic policy modifications only about once each year. So if there is a conflict between the monetary and fiscal policy authorities, the monetary authorities can move much more quickly.

Although all of these differences in policy tools, goals, models, and timing can in theory be built into game frameworks and analyzed, relatively little work has been done on this. The main reason is that the work is still complicated and difficult. Furthermore, in order to encompass all the complexities of game theory, it is usually necessary to give up the analysis of uncertainty.

As a result, the common practice at the moment is to consider a single decision maker. This lumps together monetary and fiscal-policy decision makers and assumes that they have common goals. In fact, the monetary and fiscal authorities do share goals. It is not really so much the FRB *versus* the President and Congress as it is the three groups working together to improve the performance of the economy.

2. The President versus Congress

There is frequently more conflict between the President and Congress than between these two and the FRB. Moreover, the conflict is not just between the President and Congress. There is also conflict between the House and the Senate and between Democrats and Republicans in each body.

While some formal analysis has been done on the conflicts between the FRB on the one hand and the President and Congress on the other hand, there is as yet very little formal modeling in the feedback framework of the conflict between the President and Congress or of the conflict between political parties in the Congress.

A story about an economist and feedback control theory illustrates the conflict between the President and Congress. A university economist who took an interest in the feedback framework and wanted to learn more about it went to the engineering school to listen to a seminar on an application of feedback control. The topic for the day was a stabilization system for a tank.

An elaborate hydraulic system allowed the body of the tank to ride smoothly over rough terrain. When the sensors on the front of the tank detected a depression under the first treads, a signal was fed back and the hydraulic system reacted within microseconds to offset the effects of the depression.

The economist was asking himself what if any relevance all of this had to inflation and unemployment. If the sensors were like the national income accounts and the hydraulic system was like fiscal policy . . . However, fiscal policy responds not in microseconds but in years and each depression gives the passengers in the economy a real jolt before the President and Congress decide to do anything about it. But maybe that is not really the most appropriate analogy . . .

Maybe the commander of the tank is the President and the driver who actuates the hydraulic system by hand is Congress. The gunner who is just along for the ride is the public. The commander sees a depression coming and shouts to the driver to press down on the hydraulic system. However, instead of pressing down immediately, the driver peers out through his viewer and shouts back that he does not see a depression coming. Meanwhile the public is experiencing a very rough ride indeed.

Part IV
Conclusions

13
Conclusions

The feedback control framework offers a new view of macroeconomic policy making. This view begins with desired paths for the economy. These paths allow one to focus on desired changes in the economy over time.

After the desired paths are chosen then weights must be selected to determine the relative priorities that are given to different desired paths. These weights reflect the fact that some political parties care more about a low unemployment rate than about a low inflation rate and that other parties are more concerned with arresting the growth of public expenditure than they are with lowering the unemployment rate. Also, weights which change over time encompass the reality that political decision makers care more about the state of the economy as an election approaches.

Taken together the desired paths and the weights provide a terrain for dialog between political decision makers and their economic advisers. The politicians articulate desired paths for the economy and priorities among these paths and the economic advisers use this information to design policies in the feedback framework.

This design work is accomplished by bringing together (1) the desired paths and weights with (2) an econometric model. The model embodies decision lags from the time of recognition of a problem until legislation is passed or other action taken to correct the problem. Also, the model contains effect lags from the time the action is taken until improvements occur in the economy. These two lags provide a dynamic structure that mimics the reality of a political economy systems that responds in a dreadfully slow fashion to problems.

Moreover, the model contains information about uncertainty in the form of shocks like oil price changes as well as uncertainty about behavioral responses to policies. In addition, the model includes measurement uncertainty to reflect the fact that economic analyst are more uncertain about some aspects of the economy than about others.

These elements of desired paths, priorities, dynamics, and uncertainty are brought together in the feedback framework. The result is set of feedback rules that determine each policy as a function of the state of the economy as measured by indicators such as the level of inflation, unemployment, and the balance-of-payments.

The importance of these rules is not so much that they provide a precise numerical recipe for determining policy, but that they put an emphasis on the notion of feedback. This notion can be used quite apart from the feedback framework to design institutions and policy mechanisms that respond quickly and smoothly to problems in the economy. In contrast, our existing policy procedures allow economic problems to become sever before any action is taken and then extreme actions are taken that sharply jerk the economy back in the other directions and frequently overshoot the target in the process. The feedback framework on the other hand puts an emphasis on quick, small, and smooth responses to problems in the economy.

In fact, we have been using feedback mechanism such as unemployment compensation for many years. So the principle of using feedback in economic policy is not new —just neglected. The principle could be used again in the design of a wide variety of economic programs that cut across political lines but that capture the idea of having an economic policy that responds quickly and smoothly to problems in the economy.

While feedback rules can be devised in a political-economy setting — quiet apart from the complexity of mathematics and computers — it is important to test the stability and relative performance of these rules in computer models. For example, not all feedback rules are stabilizing. The Gramm-Rudman legislation which can be viewed as a feedback rule for balancing the budget. It may well have been destabilizing. Secondly, feedback rules that use a variety of indicators such as inflation, unemployment, and the balance-of-payments may be more efficient that simpler rules that use only the unemployment rate for feedback.

We have been experiencing a rough ride in the U.S. economy in recent years. Some of that rough ride was not necessary. Feedback rules could have smoothed the ride somewhat by providing frequent, quick, and small corrections to problems rather than infrequent, slow, and large policy changes.

Notes

Chapter 2 Feedback: A Familiar Idea

Lester Thurow has pointed out that some automatic stabilizers may also make it more difficult to get back to a desired path once away from it. For example, if the unemployment rate were too low and government expenditures were cut to increase unemployment, the unemployment compensation scheme would work to make it more difficult to get back to the desired (and in this case higher) levels of unemployment. This problem will not occur with optimally derived feedback rules since the rule will attempt to return the economy to the desired path.

Chapter 3 Goals

For a discussion of desired paths and weights in macroeconomic policy see Pindyck (1973a). I am indebted to A. J. Hughes Hallet for suggesting the point about weights changing with circumstance and the level of activity.

Chapter 4 Dynamics

Both the decision and the effect lag include "recognition" lags, that is, the time from a change in the economy until the change is recognized. In the decision lag the recognition lag is the time until policy advisers recognize the change in the economy. In the effect lag the recognition lag is the time until consumers and producers realize that policies have been changed. For a historical example of the recognition lag see pp. 8-11 of Tinsley, Garrett, and Friar (1978).

Lester Thurow suggested the use of three rather than two types of lags. In his scheme the decision lag of this book is divided into (1) a decision lag and (2) a policy change lag.

For a discussion of the effect lag in macroeconomic models see Kuh and Schmalensee (1973). The dichotomy between state variables and control variables is used in the macroeconomic model context in Pindyck (1973a).

Chapter 5 Uncertainty

For macroeconomic models with shock uncertainty see Bray (1974), Garbade (1975), and Wall and Westcott (1974). For a macroeconomic model with shock, behavioral, and measurement uncertainties see Kendrick (1982).

Chapter 6 Feedback Rules

The first numerical application of quadratic-linear control theory to macroeconomic problems in the United States was by Pindyck (1973a) and (1973b). Some textbooks on control theory are Aoki (1967) and (1976), Athans and Falb (1966), Bryson and Ho (1969), Chow (1975) and (1981), Kendrick (1981), and Pitchford and

Turnovsky (1977).

Some applications of control theory to macroeconomic models in which there is behavioral uncertainty are Cooper and Fischer (1975), Craine (1979), and Shupp (1972).

Chapter 7 Confidence Intervals Again

For a technical discussion of confidence intervals over time see Bar-Shalom (1977). The ellipses in Figure 7.4 and 7.5 are a special case of the more general confidence ellipse that would have axes which are not horizontal and vertical. For a discussion see Theil (1971), p. 134.

Chapter 8 Automatic Stabilizers Revisited

For examples of the application of feedback control methods to agriculture see Arzac and Wilkinson (1979) and Rausser (1978).

Chapter 9 Choice of Criterion

For deterministic macroeconomic models with a variety of criterion functions see Craine, Havenner, and Tinsley (1976), Drud (1976), Fair (1974), Livesey (1971), Turnovsky (1979), and Melliss (1984). A description of the asymmetric quadratic criterion function is given in Friedman (1972). For one exchange about the proper form of the criterion function in deterministic problems see the article by Palash (1977) and the comments by Livesey (1977) and Shupp (1977). For a description of an iterative method for determining the weights in a quadratic criterion function see Rustem, Velupillai, and Westcott (1978). For other discussions of the criterion see Bray (1982), p. 34, and Tinsley and von Zur Muehlen(1981).

Chapter 10 Reactions to Policy

For a discussion of rational expectations see Sargent and Wallace (1976) and Lucas (1976) and for a discussion of policy inconsistency see Kydland and Prescott (1977). For an example of a recent paper on reactions to rules see Karakitsos and Rustem (1984). For methods of estimating models with rational expectations see Chow (1980), Hansen and Sargent (1980), and Taylor (1979). For descriptions and applications of active learning control methods where estimation and control are combined to include probing see Norman (1976), Prescott (1972), Tse and Bar-Shalom (1973), and Kendrick (1982).

The situation in which both the government and consumers try to anticipate the other's response is like a conjectural varaiation as discussed in Brandsma and Hughes Hallet (1984).

Chapter 11 The Choice of Model

For a method of pooling information from models see Rustem (1985) and for an approach to selecting the best feedback rule to use see Chow (1977) and Rustem (1985). An alternative approach to the choice of model is in Section III.A of Kalchbrenner and Tinsley with Berry and Garrett (1977).

Notes

Chapter 12 Multiple Decision Makers

One of the first studies on multiple decision makers in macroeconomic policy was Pindyck (1976). Some recent papers on dynamic games are Cansever, Basar and Cruz (1984), Taylor (1984), Miller (1985), Carraro (1985), and Pindyck and Neese(1984).

References

Aoki, Masanao (1967), *Optimization of Stochastic Systems*, Academic Press, New York.

______ (1976), *Dynamic Economic Theory and Control in Economics*, American Elsevier, New York.

Arzac, Enrique R., and Maurice Wilkinson (1979), "Stabilization Policies for United States Feed Grain and Livestock Markets," *Journal of Economic Dynamics and Control*, Vol. 1, No. 1, pp. 39-58.

Athans, Michael, and Peter L. Falb (1966), *Optimal Control*, McGraw-Hill, New York.

Bar-Shalom, Yaakov (1977), "Effects of Uncertainties on the Control Performance of Linear Systems with Unknown Parameters and Trajectory Confidence Tubes", *Annals of Economic and Social Measurement*, Volume 6, No. 5, Winter-Spring, 1977/78, pp. 599-612.

Brandsma, Andries, and A. J. Hughes Hallet (1984), "Economic Conflict and the Solution of Dynamic Games", *European Economic Review*, Vol. 26, pp. 13-32.

Bray, Jeremy (1974), "Predictive Control of a Stochastic Model of the U.K. Economy Simulating Present Policy Making Practice by the U.K. Government," *Annals of Economic and Social Measurement*, Vol. 3, No.1, January, pp. 239-56.

______ (1982), *Production, Purpose and Structure*, Frances Pinter (Publishers), London.

Bryson, Arthur E., Jr., and Yu-Chi Ho (1969), *Applied Optimal Control*, Blaisdell, Waltham, Mass.

Cansever, D., T. Basar, and J. B. Cruz Jr. (1984), "Robustness of Incentive Policies in Team Problems with Discrepancies in Goal Perceptions," pp. 281-288 in T. Basar and L. F. Pau (eds), *Dynamic Modellling and Control of National Economies 1983*, Pergamon Press, Oxford, England.

Carraro, Carlo (1985), "Optimal Economic Policy Determination: From Control to Game Theory," presented at the International Conference of Economic Policies and Control Theory, University of Venice, Venice, Italy, January.

Chow, Gregory C. (1975), *Analysis and Control of Dynamic Systems*, John Wiley and Sons, Inc., New York.

______ (1977), "Usefulness of Imperfect Models for the Formulation of Stabilization Policies," *Annals of Economic and Social Measurement*, Vol. 6, No.2, Spring, pp. 175-188.

References

______ (1980), "Estimation of Rational Expectations Models", *Journal of Economic Dynamics and Control*, Vol. 2, No. 3, August, pp. 241-256.

______ (1981), *Econometric Analysis by Control Methods*, John Wiley and Sons, Inc., New York.

Cooper, J. Phillips, and Stanley Fischer (1975), "A Method for Stochastic Control of Nonlinear Econometric Models and an Application", *Econometrica*, Vol. 4, No.1, January, pp.147-162.

Craine, Roger (1979), "Optimal Monetary Policy with Uncertainty", *Journal of Economic Dynamics and Control*, Vol. 1, No. 1, February, pp.59-84.

Craine, Roger, Arthur Havenner, and Peter Tinsley (1976), "Optimal Macroeconomic Control Policies", *Annals of Economic and Social Measurement*, Vol. 5, No. 2, Spring, pp. 191-203.

Drud, Arne (1976), *Methods for Control of Complex Dynamic Systems*, Institute for Mathematical Statistics and Operations Research, Technical University of Denmark, No. 27.

Fair, Ray C. (1974), "On the Solution of Optimal Control Problems As Maximization Problems", *Annals of Economic and Social Measurement*, Vol. 3, No. 1, January, pp. 135-154.

Friedman, Benjamin M. (1972), "Optimal Economic Stabilization Policy: An Extended Framework," *Journal of Political Economy*, Vol. 80, September-October, pp. 1002-1022.

Garbade, Kenneth D. (1975), *Discretionary Control of Aggregate Economic Activity*, Lexington, Lexington, Mass.

Hansen, Lars Peter, and Thomas J. Sargent (1980), "Formulating and Estimating Dynamic Linear Rational Expectations Models", *Journal of Economic Dynamics and Control*, Vol. 2, No. 1, February, pp. 7-46.

Karakitsos, E., and B. Rustem (1984), "Optimally Derived Fixed Rules and Indicators,", *Journal of Economic Dynamics and Control*, Vol. 8, No. 1, October, pp. 33-64.

Kalchbrenner, J. H., and P. A. Tinsley with J. Berry and B. Garrett (1977), "On Filtering Auxiliary Information in Short-Run Monetary Policy," in K. Brunner and A. Meltzer (eds), *Optimal Policies, Capital Theory, and Technology Exports*, North Holland Publishing Co. Amsterdam, pp. 39-84.

Kendrick, David A. (1981), *Stochastic Control for Economic Models*, McGraw-Hill Book Company, New York.

______ (1982), "Caution and Probing in a Macroeconomic Model," *Journal of Economic Dynamics and Control*, Vol. 4, No. 2, May, pp. 149-170.

References

Kydland, Finn and Edward C. Prescott (1977), "Rules Rather than Discretion: The Inconsistency of Optimal Plans," *Journal of Political Economy*, Vol. 85, pp.473-491.

Kuh, Edwin, and Richard L. Schmalensee (1973), *An Introduction to Applied Macroeconomics*, North Holland Publishing Co., Amsterdam.

Lucas, Robert E., Jr. (1976), "Econometric Policy Evaluation: A Critique," in *The Phillips Curve and Labor Markets*, K. Brunner and A. H. Meltzer (eds.), North-Holland Publishing Co., Amsterdam, pp. 19-46.

Livesey, David A. (1971), "Optimizing Short Term Economic Policy", *Economic Journal*, Volume 81, pp. 525-546.

______ (1977), "Comment", *Annals of Economic and Social Measurement*, Vol. 6, No. 3, Summer, pp. 291-293.

Melliss, C. L. (1984), "Some Experiments with Optimal Control on the Treasury Model," Government Economic Service Working Paper No. 67, HM Treasury, Parliament Street, London SW1P 3AG.

Miller, Marcus (1985), "Policy Coordination and Dynamic Games," presented at the International Conference of Economic Policies and Control Theory, University of Venice, Venice, Italy, January.

Norman, Alfred L. (1976), "First Order Dual Control", *Annals of Economic and Social Measurement*, Vol. 5, No. 3, Spring, pp. 311-322.

Palash, Carl J. (1977), "On the Specification of Unemployment and Inflation in the Objective Function," *Annals of Economic and Social Measurement*, Vol. 6, No. 3, Summer, pp. 275-290.

Pindyck, Robert S. (1973a), *Optimal Planning for Economic Stabilization*, North-Holland Publishing Co., Amsterdam.

______ (1973b), "Optimal Policies for Economic Stabilization," *Econometrica*, Vol. 41, No. 3, pp. 529-560, May.

______ (1976), "The Cost of Conflicting Objectives in Policy Formulation," *Annals of Economic and Social Measurement*, Vol. 5, No. 2, pp. 239-248.

______ and J. W. Neese (1984), "Behavioral Assumptions in Decentralized Stabilization Policies," Ch. 12 in A. J. Hughes Hallet (ed), *Applied Decision Analysis and Economic Behavior*, Martinus Nijhoff Publishers, Dordrecht, The Netherlands.

Pitchford, John and Stephen Turnovsky (1977), *Applications of Control Theory to Economic Analysis*, North-Holland Publishing Co., Amsterdam.

References

Prescott, Edward C. (1972), "The Multi-Period Control Problem under Uncertainty", *Econometrica*, Vol. 40, pp. 1043-1058.

Rausser, Gordon (1978), "Active Learning, Control Theory, and Agricultural Policy," *American Journal of Agricultural Economics*, Vol. 60, No. 3, pp. 476-490.

Rustem, Berc (1985), "Methods for Simultaneous Use of Multiple Models in Optimal Policy Design," presented at the International Conference of Economic Policies and Control Theory, University of Venice, Venice, Italy, January.

______, K. Velupillai, and J. H. Westcott (1978), "Respecifying the Weighting Matrix of a Quadratic Objective Function," *Automatica*, Vol. 14, pp. 567-582.

Sargent, Thomas J., and Neil Wallace (1976), "Rational Expectations and the Theory of Economic Policy," *Journal of Monetary Economics*, Vol. 2, pp. 169-184.

Shupp, Franklin R. (1972), "Uncertainty and Stabilization Policies for a Nonlinear Macroeconomic Model", *Quarterly Journal of Economics*, Vol. 80, No. 1, February, pp. 94-110.

______ (1977), "Comment," *Annals of Economic and Social Measurement*, Vol. 6, No. 3, Summer, pp. 295-300.

Taylor, John B. (1979), "Estimation and Control of a Macroeconomic Model with Rational Expectations", *Econometrica*, Vol. 47, No. 5, pp. 1267-1286.

______ (1984), "International Coordination in the Design of Macroeconomic Policy Rules," Working Paper No. 1506, National Bureau of Economic Research, Cambridge, Mass.

Theil, Henri (1971), *Principles of Econometrics*, John Wiley and Sons, Inc., New York.

Tinsley P. A., B. Garrett, and M. E. Friar (1978), "The Measurement of Money Demand," Federal Reserve Board Special Studies Paper No. 133.

______ and P. von zur Muehlen (1981), "A Maximum Probability Approach to Short-Run Policy," *Journal of Econometrics*, Vol. 15, pp. 31-48.

Turnovsky, Stephen J. (1979), "Optimal Monetary Policy under Flexible Exchange Rates," *Journal of Economic Dynamics and Control*, Vol. 1, No. 1, February, pp. 85-100.

Tse, Edison, and Yaakov Bar-Shalom (1973), "An Actively Adaptive Control for Linear Systems with Random Parameters," *IEEE Transactions on Automatic Control*, AC-18, April, pp. 109-117.

Wall K.D., and J. H. Westcott (1974), "Macroeconomic Modeling for Control," *IEEE Transactions on Automatic Control*, AC-19, December, pp. 862-873.

Index

Index

Index

Index

Index

ADVANCED STUDIES IN THEORETICAL AND APPLIED ECONOMETRICS

---

1. Paelinck J.H.P. (ed.): Qualitative and Quantitative Mathematical Economics, 1982.
   ISBN 90 247 2623 9.
2. Ancot J.P. (ed.): Analysing the Structure of Economic Models, 1984.
   ISBN 90 247 2894 0.
3. Hughes Hallett A.J. (ed.): Applied Decision Analysis and Economic Behaviour, 1984.
   ISBN 90 247 2968 8.
4. Sengupta J.K.: Information and Efficiency in Economic Decision, 1985.
   ISBN 90 247 3072 4.
5. Artus P. and Guvenen O., in collaboration with Gagey F. (eds.): International Macroeconomic Modelling for Policy Decisions, 1986.
   ISBN 90 247 3201 8.
6. Vilares M.J.: Structural Change in Macroeconomic Models, 1986.
   ISBN 90 247 3277 8.
7. Carraro C. and Sartore D. (eds.): Developments of Control Theory for Economic Analysis, 1987.
   ISBN 90 247 3345 6.
8. Broer D.P. (ed.): Neoclassical Theory and Empirical Models of Aggregate Firm Behaviour, 1987.
   ISBN 90 247 3412 6.
9. Italianer A. (ed.): Theory and Practice of International Trade Linkage Models, 1986.
   ISBN 90 247 3407 X.
10. Kendrick D.A.: Feedback, 1988.
    ISBN 90 247 3593 9 (HB). ISBN 90 247 3650 1 (PB).
11. Sengupta J.K. and Kadekodi G.K. (eds.): Econometrics of Planning and Efficiency, 1988.
    ISBN 90 247 3602 1.
12. Griffith D.A.: Advanced Spatial Statistics, 1988.
    ISBN 90 247 3627 7.